TRUCK TALK

Chilton Book Company
Philadelphia • New York • Londo

Montie Tak

TRUCK TALK

The language of the open road

First Edition

Published in Philadelphia by Chilton Book Company
and simultaneously in Ontario, Canada,
by Thomas Nelson & Sons, Ltd.

ISBN: 0-8019-5642-0

Library of Congress Catalog Card Number 72-169583

Manufactured in the United States of America

Designed by Adrianne Onderdonk Dudden

To my Mother, for all her loving guidance;

To the cherished memory of my Father;

To Jack, for his patient teaching.

I couldn't have done it without you.

Acknowledgments

There are certain people whose teaching, selfless interest and encouragement have been instrumental in the compilation of this work.

I wish to thank Professor W. R. Bowden of Dickinson College, for whose English class this work originally appeared as a three-page paper. If he had not taken the time and patience to listen to me, this book might not have been.

My deepest thanks must go to Agnes Grant and Alice Feuerstein of the New York Public School System for encouraging my interest in the English language by their exemplary teaching, and to Sebastian Haskel, who very early showed me the essence of meticulous scholarship.

I owe a large debt of thanks to the operators and management of Daily Express, Inc., for their patience, advice and cooperation in helping me gather material during my employment at Daily.

And I thank the many truckers everywhere who do not expect thanks but who took the time and the interest to contribute to this book.

The next cup of coffee is on me.

Montie Tak

Introduction

Much of the flavor and tempo of the life of an occupational group is reflected in its speech. Emerson once said: "I confess to some pleasure from the stinging rhetoric of a rattling oath in the mouths of truckmen and teamsters. . . . Cut these words and they would bleed; they are vascular and alive; they walk and run." Although he was referring to the original horse-driving teamsters and truckers, his comments are true of the speech used by our motorized truck drivers of almost one hundred years later.

Somewhere on the roads of our country, the in-language shared by this society on wheels became "truck talk," a language by and large unheard by the public, and ignored by those doing research in the field of language and slang. When I first became interested in trucks and truckers, I became aware of the lack of information on the subject, and the absence of printed materials led me to the primary source of the language: the truckers themselves. Fortunately, while a student, I was working after classes at the office of a trucking company and had ample opportunity to talk with operators and drivers, as well as to examine first-hand the tractors which were their pride and the different kinds of equipment they used. Then, too, I had several acquaintances in the industry who drove for other companies and could supply me with information on the many different facets of trucking to which I did not have access. My main source of information, however, remained the drivers of the company I worked for. I consider the vocabulary I have compiled to be a fair representation of the language used by truckers in the United States, because my informants were long-distance drivers who came into contact with truckers from all parts of the country.

In the course of my early search, I found that the more I asked questions the more I had to ask. Part of this progression was the result of my expanding desire to know more about trucks, and part of it could be attributed to the fact that when I asked a trucker what double-clutching was, or to explain the mysterious rites performed by dollies or by a triplex transmission, his answer was as incomprehensible to me as the subject of the original question. Certainly the response sounded like English, and written down it even looked like English, but I couldn't understand it. Analyzed word by word, the meanings were far different from what they seemed to be when grouped in a phrase or sentence, and the reason for that is simple: the men of the road have a language specifically structured to cope with difficulties of communication within their occupational group.

Truck drivers in general are not overly given to ceremony. In the course of daily events, the words they use are explicit, concise, colorful and expressive, and they have evolved to fulfill a distinct purpose: speed and ease of communication. It is to be carefully noted that truck talk is not slang but a language of expediency. The technical words in the vocabulary usually express an idea that expressed in any other way would require lengthy explanations, and working men have little time and less need for such. There are few formal words in truck talk because there are few formal truckers.

The outstanding characteristic of the terms is that they represent a fresh way of looking at things that is concrete, colorful and often humorous. It is worthy of note, too, that truck talk is remarkably clean-minded, having relatively few terms with connotations at all sexual or obscene.

The words that compose truck talk are the verbal cement which helps to hold together a group of people whose profession demands incessant travel and consequently evokes a feeling of being alone. Truckers need to be recognizably one with their fellows when they do congregate at truck stops and terminals: similarities of dress and speech patterns serve to reinforce group identification and to strengthen camaraderie among strangers. As a result, truckers are a close-knit group whose members hold common attitudes and discuss them with a common language. The words themselves are drawn from the context of everyday life, and have both social and grammatical origins. They may satisfy a function such as a description of technical processes; they may exhibit the social aspects of the role of the trucker or be self-descriptive; they may be traditional words that have acquired new or revised meanings. Many trucking terms must have developed from a humorous interpretation of events in the course of a day's work. Two truckers who operate the same rig together may be said to be "married"; the same men, when they no longer drive with each other, are "divorced." A short driver who experienced difficulty in getting into and out of his lofty cabover tractor would have nicknamed it a "peach picker" and another trucker whose ears rang from the din made by his noisy truck naturally called his rig a "cement mixer." Some anonymous, sleepy long-haul driver must have been the first to ask a waitress for a cup of "hundred-mile coffee."

Truckers often describe themselves or others by what they haul. The result is such terminology as "gravy hauler," "painted scrap-iron hauler," "shanty shifter," "sand hacker," "bed-bug hauler" and "suicide jockey." If a man drives for "Pork Chop Express," he hauls hogs, naturally. Another mode of description hints at the type of operation maintained or the sort of driving behavior exhibited, such as "clutch artist," "believer," "lead-foot," "wildcat," "truck-stop commando," and "aviator."

There is little or no possibility that the meanings of the words I have recorded will remain the same or stay regionalized for the simple reason that new coinages and new meanings for older terms span the continent as rapidly as the big rigs their users drive. Language is, after all, the creation of the people who use it. Variations in the meanings of the same words often exist, as well as a great number of synonyms for driving fast, downshifting, low gear, high gear, going downhill in neutral, applying the brakes, making a turn, the different makes and types of tractors and trailors, and the truckers themselves. In most cases I have provided synonyms or cross-references that represent related or contrasting terms.

As commercial innovations and new types of trucks take over in this growing industry, we can be assured that truck drivers will create and spread new terms, for truck talk is a language in flux and a mirror of a special way of life and of social change. With the increasing presence of containerized cargoes, for instance, the names "fishyback," "birdyback" and "piggyback" have arisen to describe their transport via ship, plane and train. As a living, changing language, truck talk adapts itself to its speakers every day in all parts of the country.

Since I first began work on this dictionary, I myself have become an owner-operator and part of the trucking community. I know that in the course of a conversation with another trucker, I use many of the terms whose meanings had me completely baffled only a few years ago, and I expect that an uninitiated listener would feel much as I did then.

Chief among my motives in compiling these words is, I would say, my own satisfaction. I wanted to write a book because there has been no previous treatment of any depth or accuracy and because I hoped to present to the reader a text which would both entertain and instruct. I am certain that the list is by no means complete and that my ignorance has caused errors in concept and phraseology. By no means do I attempt to act as spokesman for the trucking industry and its people. I welcome amendments and criticism, but I will be more than rewarded if another who is as yet uninitiated into, or still fascinated by, the world of gear jammers and their big rigs gains insight into the way of life that has captivated me.

TRUCK TALK

A

A-car: short for Autocar, a make of over-the-road tractor. Once known as the "Hercules of Trucks," the Autocar is less frequently seen today because of the rising popularity of the cabover tractor (A-cars are conventional cabs) and because White Motors, which bought out Autocar in 1953, has concentrated on its White Division for its long-haul tractors.
Syn.: Awful-car.

air bag: a device on tag axles that utilizes air pressure in the suspension system.
Cf. air ride, air tag.

air bound: said of a truck when it runs out of fuel or when air blocks the fuel lines and prevents fuel added to the tanks from passing through.
Cf. bleed the fuel lines.

air brakes: a brake system in a vehicle that depends on air pressure to activate the brakes by means of diaphragms, diaphragms and wedges, or cams and levers.
Cf. low-air warning device, push 'n' wonder brakes.

air hose: the connection between the tractor and the trailer that supplies air to the trailer's brakes.
Cf. blow him up, charge a trailer, handshake, pogo stick, trolley lines.

air-lift axle: an axle with an elevating device operated by air that enables the trucker to regulate the amount of weight carried on that axle by raising or lowering it. An air lift is common on rigs with five or more axles; it can be any axle but is most commonly the rearmost axle of the tractor or the foremost axle of the trailer. On a tandem spread trailer, the foremost axle usually operates on an air lift. On turns, the driver deactivates it so that the duals clear the ground, preventing a dragging effect on the axle. The driver can also deactivate the air lift when deadheading to save on tire wear.

Cf. air ride, air tag, cheater axle, three-legged trailer.

air-over-hydraulic brakes: brakes on a vehicle that have a regular hydraulic system assisted by an air pressure system.

Cf. air brakes, push 'n' wonder brakes.

air pressure gauge: a gauge on the tractor dash that indicates the pounds of air pressure in the air system.

Cf. low-air warning devices.

air ride: an air ride tractor is equipped with an air bag on each wheel to cushion and smooth out the ride. Such a tractor has no rear springs, but the air bags absorb the shock. This method has the advantage over steel springs because the former have less weight, cost less to maintain, and have a lower initial cost.

Cf. air tag, bone crusher.

air slider: a cab-controlled sliding fifth wheel that can be unlocked by air to be moved backward or forward.

Syn.: slider.

Cf. fifth wheel.

air tag: a tag axle that has two bellows-like air bags that, when filled, force the tractor's rear axle harder against the ground for a smoother ride. An air tag is also used to compensate the weight distribution of the two axles of the tractor. Sometimes a tandem spread trailer with a steering axle in the rear has an air tag for the same reason.

Cf. air ride, tag axle.

all dolled up: said of a tractor with a customized paint job and accessories, such as chrome trim and pinstripes.

Syn.: decked out.

Cf. floating chrome, goodied up, hillbilly chrome, rolling palace, zebra stripes.

alligator: an old-time cabover tractor that lacked the tilt-cab mechanism for easy access to the engine. The mechanic had to burrow headfirst into the interior of the engine from the driver's compartment. These cabovers were called alligators because they looked as if they were about to swallow the intrepid trucker or garageman.

Cf. flip top, two-story Emeryville.

all stretched out: said of a truck driven at its top speed.

Syn.: big hole it, build a fire, floorboard it, gettin' stretched, highball it, pour on the coals, tacked out.

Cf. clean his clock, dust 'em off, smoke him.

American Trucking Association, Inc.: the national

association of fifty-one state trucking associations and thirteen various conferences of different classes of motor carriers and haulers. The organization distributes publications for drivers, such as *Facts for Drivers* and *Revised Safety Regulations,* and produces "good will" literature on trucks for public consumption. In addition, the association sponsors the annual National Truck Roadeo, which recognizes and awards the nation's most expert drivers.

Cf. P.U.C. Roadeo.

anchor: to apply the brakes.

Syn.: clamp on the binders, grab a handful of air, throw out the anchor.

Cf. anchors.

anchors: the brakes of a truck.

Syn.: binders, cinchers.

Cf. Emma Jesse brake, jack-off bar, Johnson bar, trolley-valve handle.

anteater: nickname for the C-model Mack tractor, which is a short-nosed conventional cab, the nose of which slants obliquely toward the ground.

Cf. B-model, cherry picker, Mack, sidewinder.

antifly device: a metal device, usually shaped like an inverted letter T, that keeps a truck's mud flaps hanging directly behind the tires.

Cf. mud flaps.

armstrong starter: a hand crank used on early trucks along with such relics as chain-drive transmissions and solid rubber tires.

Syn.: stem winder, stew winder.

Cf. crank, give her the works, shake down the ashes.

Autocar: a make with conventional cabs; because of the vogue of cabover tractors in over-the-road use, Autocars are mainly used in off-the-road applications, such as concrete mixers and dump trucks.
Syn.: A-car, awful-car.

aux box: the auxiliary gear box, which is the mechanism that determines the level of speed available for each gear in the main box. The purpose of an auxiliary transmission is to enable a closer splitting of the gear ratio. An aux box has two, three or four speeds and can be used in combination with a main box of four or five speeds. In most instances, if the aux box has two speeds its gear stick is located to the right of the one for the main box. If it is a three- or four-speed box, the stick is located in front of the one for the main box and is equally accessible for the driver.
Cf. brownie, duplex, gearboxes, mixing stick, quadriplex, Roadranger, triplex, two-stick transmission.

aviator: a speeding driver.
Syn.: highballer, lead foot.
Cf. cowboy, grounded, Sears-Roebuck license.

awful-car: synonym for Autocar.

axle: the bar or axle-tree that connects opposite wheels. There are two kinds of axles: live axles, which transmit power from the drive shaft to the wheels, and dead axles, which do not transmit power and are used only to help carry the load or steer.
Cf. air tag, drivers, pusher, steer axle, trail axle.

axle back: said of the steering axle on a tractor when it is set back for the maximum transfer of the tractor's weight forward.
Cf. axle forward, cab forward.

axle forward: said of the steering axle on a tractor when it is located in an extreme forward position (on conventional cabs) enabling the tractor to haul the maximum load in states with a bridge formula load restriction.
Cf. axle back, axle weight, cab forward, stretch out, West Coast rig, West Coast tandem.

axle out a load: to weigh or scale out a load to ascertain the gross combination weight and the weight per axle of the tractor-trailer.
Cf. axle weight, **G.C.W.**, **G.V.W.**, on behind, over on the drive.

axle shift: to change the axle speed in a tractor that has a two- or three-speed rear axle.
Cf. five-and-two, idiot transmission.

axle weight: the amount of a rig's gross weight that rests on any one axle.
Cf. axle out a load, over on the drive.

B

babymoon hubcaps: small, round chrome hubcaps.
Cf. Budd wheels, square wheels.

back haul: the return load a trucker hauls from his first destination to a second or back to his point of origin.
Cf. flyer, turn.

back off: to let up on the throttle because otherwise the rig will windmill.

Cf. brakin' 'er down, lugging, overspeed, tacked out, windmill.

back-pasture hauler: a trucker who makes a practice of running back roads and small two-lane highways.

Cf. boondockin', four-laner, hot load, moonlighter.

baffle: **1.** longitudinal and latitudinal compartment walls in a tanker trailer that keep the load from slopping forward or backward when the driver slows or stops the rig. **2.** the interior components of the muffler on an exhaust stack that reduce the amount of noise the engine makes.

Cf. gutted, smitty, smokestack, spittoon muffler, twin chimneys.

balloon freight: light, bulky cargo.

Syn.: load of wind, zephyr haul.

Cf. load of sand, load of suds, feather hauler, smoker, swinger.

baloneys: truck tires.

Syn.: rubber, skins.

Cf. cheater slicks, duals, irons, micks, pumpkin, rider, waffles.

bandaged up: said of a tractor with any impromptu winter front. A trucker often uses road maps, Navajo blankets, tape, corrugated cardboard or whatever is available in an effort to keep the truck's interior warm.

Cf. bandaids, diapers, winter front.

bandaids: an impromptu winter front on a tractor.

Syn.: diapers.
Cf. bandaged up, fair-weather driver.

banger: a diesel engine cylinder; the term is usually preceded by a number that stands for the number of cylinders in the engine. For instance, a six-banger is a diesel engine with six cylinders.
Cf. four-lunger.

banjo: the differential housing on a drive axle.
Syn.: pot.
Cf. pig, rear end assembly.

bar ditch: the shoulder of the road. Used in Texas and the Southwest; rarely heard anywhere else. Perhaps a contraction of "barrow ditch."
Syn.: barrow ditch.
Cf. berm, buy up an orchard, dusting.

bareback: said of a tractor less its semi-trailer.
Syn.: bobtail, loose horse, solo.
Cf. drop the box, unlatch.

barefoot: refers to a tractor or trailer that lacks one or more tires.
Cf. racin' slicks, rider.

bark: to produce a loud, hearty growling sound; said of the smokestacks. This is in special reference to a Mack tractor, whose trademark is a bulldog.
Cf. talk.

barrel on down the road: to drive a truck at high speed.
Syn.: build a fire, burn the breeze, flyin' low, haul the mail, highball it, lean on it, open 'er up, pour it on, run wide open, tacked out.
Cf. keep 'er winding, smokin' in high gear.

barrow ditch: the edge or shoulder of the road. Apparently indigenous to Texas and the Southwest; rarely heard elsewhere.
Syn.: bar ditch.
Cf. berm, buy up an orchard, dusting.

basket case: an abandoned tractor that has had most of its original equipment stripped off or stolen.
Cf. strip her.

bathtub dump: an aluminum dump trailer; so named because of its resemblance to a bathtub.
Cf. bottom dumps, hungry boards, tipper, water-level hauling capacity.

B.B.C.: the length of the tractor from the **b**umper to the **b**ack of the **c**ab. This measurement is always given in inches.

beach: to stop a truck or coast to a parking place.
Cf. brakin' 'er down, set her down, spike it.

beam trailer: a lowboy trailer that lacks a solid floor but has beams for the machinery or other cargo to rest on.
Cf. detachable gooseneck, outriggers.

beaned up: bennied up.
Cf. bennie, copilots, eye trouble, Upjohns, West Coast turnaround.

bean hauler: a trucker who transports dry food products.
Cf. garbage hauler, gravy hauler, iron hauler, meat hauler, shoat and goat conductor, weeder geese hauler.

Bean Town: Boston.
Cf. Big Town, Chi, Dago.

bedbug hauler: a trucker who drives a moving van.

Syn.: relocation consultant.

Cf. household goods mover, house number hunters, mountain climbin' job.

bedsteader: a sleepy driver who cannot be depended on to stay awake on night runs and who is probably in constant search of hundred-mile coffee.

Cf. eye trouble, pull a sleep job, put to sleep, roll and rest.

been around the Horn: said of a tractor that has accumulated a high mileage; not necessarily but possibly a gunny sack job, depending on the skill and conscientiousness of its drivers.

Cf. bucket of bolts, crate, junker, residenter.

believer: a trucker who obeys all rules and regulations of the road.

Cf. aviator, cowboy, run legal, tailboard artist, vulture.

belly: a livestock trailer with a drop frame.

Syn.: pot belly, possum belly.

Cf. bull rack.

belly dump: a trailer that has gates in the floor through which it is unloaded.

Syn.: bottom dump.

belly up: to turn a truck over in a wreck.

Cf. buy up an orchard, jackknife, pile up, total it out.

belt drive: a tag axle driven by V-belts, which transmit power from the drive axle.

Syn.: rubber band drive.

Cf. bogies, drivers, powered by rubber bands, pusher, two axles pulling.

bennie: short for Benzedrine, a drug of the stimulant family and one of the stay-awake aids used occasionally (and extralegally) by some drivers.

Note: Bennies are often jokingly referred to as "brother Ben," "my good friend Benjamin," "better let Bennie drive," "copilot Ben."

Syn.: helpers.

Cf. copilots, L.A. turnaround, Upjohns.

bennie chaser: coffee a trucker carries in a thermos.

Cf. copilots, helpers, hundred-mile coffee.

berm: the shoulder of the road, that part which is between the highway and the ditch.

Cf. barrow ditch, buy up an orchard, dusting.

between the fence rows: in lane, where a driver tries to keep his truck.

Cf. buy up an orchard.

bible: **1.** the Interstate Commerce Commission's regulations book on trucking, driver and equipment standards. **2.** a book of road maps, an atlas.

Cf. brain bag.

bid run: in a company, a regular run over a specific route to the same terminal or destination. A bid run gets its name from the fact that all the company's drivers make periodic bids to determine which runs they get.

Cf. relay, roving team.

Bifocal International: a cabover tractor of limited vintage manufactured by International Harvester in 1960; so named because the cab had two small windows, one on each side, at the floor level of the interior. The purpose of the windows was to make it easy for the driver to judge distances between the tractor and other objects or vehicles nearby. These tractors were used mostly in terminals and freight yards where exact maneuvering is required.

Cf. corn binder, Emeryville, spaceship, two-story Emeryville, West Coast binder.

Note: It is said (jocularly) that the driver of a Bifocal International must wear huaraches so that his big toes can see where they are going.

big hat: a state trooper.

Cf. bird dog, bubble gum machine, cop caller, cop spotters, Radar Alley, whistlin' gear, vulture.

big hole: the gear shift position for the highest combination of gears in the tractor's transmission.

Syn.: go-home hole, pay hole, whistlin' gear.

Cf. creeper gear, grandma gear, wobbly hole.

big hole it: to drive a truck at top speed; often used in making up for lost time.

Syn.: floorboard it, highball it, pour on the coals.

Cf. big hole.

big rig: a tractor-trailer combination.

Syn.: combination, rig, semi, tandem, tractor-trailer, widow-maker.

Cf. big rig man, truck.

big rigger: an arrogant trucker, esp. one who will drive only the longest or biggest rigs.

Cf. aviator, cowboy, highballer, sheep herder, tailboard artist, truck jockey.

big rig man: a trucker; a man who drives a tractor-trailer.
Syn.: double-clutchin' man, gear shifter, semi-driver.

Big Town: New York City.
Cf. Bean Town, Chi, Frisco, Dago, L.A.

bill of lading: a document that specifies the contents of a cargo and the terms and conditions under which the goods are to be transported.
Cf. bulk freight, L.T.L., minnie, tariff.

billy goat: the 318 hp Detroit diesel engine.
Cf. Detroit diesel, Hillbilly Special.

binders: **1.** a truck's brakes.
Syn.: anchors, cinchers.
Cf. clamp on the binders.
2. the clamps used to secure the chains holding a payload on a lowboy or flat bed trailer.
Cf. boomer, boom it down, button her up, chains and binders, cheater bar.

bird dog: the chaser car of a two-man radar team, the trooper who "retrieves" a speeding trucker.
Cf. big hat, bubble gum machine, cop spotters, Radar Alley, whistlin' gear, vulture.

bird feeder: the air-intake pipe and its cover which provides the engine with air for combustion. It is called a bird feeder because of its appearance.
Syn.: breather.
Cf. bonnet, Redwood Tree.

birdyback: the practice of shipping loaded trailers on airplanes.
Cf. containerization, fishyback, piggyback.

bite a turn: to cut a corner.
Syn.: chop a turn, split-arc.
Cf. need a hinge, wrap 'er around the bend.

bleed the air tanks: to drain the accumulated water out of the air tanks of a tractor to prevent the condensed water from reducing air capacity and thus cutting braking efficiency.

bleed the fuel lines: to remove any accumulated air from the fuel lines.
Cf. air bound, ether lock.

blimp: a short, high trailer.
Cf. box, pup, semi.

blind side: the right side of a tractor-trailer.
Cf. spot mirror, West Coast mirrors.

blower: **1.** a device that forces additional air into the engine to increase its efficiency and horsepower. Two types of blowers are the supercharger or turbocharger. **2.** a fan that blows air over ice to maintain a low temperature in a trailer transporting perishable goods.
Cf. bunker, putt-putt, reefer.

blow him up: to give a tractor equipped with an air starter an air "transfusion" to build up the air pressure in the tractor. This is done to enable the trucker to start his tractor if the latter has lost all its air, and is accomplished by connecting the respective glad hands (air hose connections) of the donor truck and the recipient truck. In the same way, a rig with an air-emergency brake may have to be "blown up" in the event that it loses its air and the brakes lock up.
Cf. gesundheit starter.

blow-off valve: a regulatory valve on the air system that allows the escape of excess air pressure if the governor on the air compressor fails to operate.

blow up: any seizure or large-scale engine failure.
Cf. broke to lead, rehaul.

blunt-nose: nickname for a cabover tractor.
Syn.: flat face, flip top, pug, snub-nose.
Cf. cabover, conventional.

B-model: the popular conventional model Mack that is so well known by sight.
Cf. anteater, cherry picker, follow the bulldog, sidewinder.

bobtail: said of a trucker when he drives a tractor without its semi-trailer, as in "runs bobtail."
Syn.: bareback, loose horse, solo.

bobtail miles: the number of miles a tractor runs bobtail, or without hauling a semi-trailer, and for which the trucker receives little or no pay.
Cf. deadhead, load of postholes.

Bob White: a flap valve that rests over the opening of the smokestack when the rig is not running.
Syn.: butterfly, woodpecker.

body: the semi-trailer, the load-carrying unit of a tractor-trailer combination.
Syn.: box, semi, tandem.
Cf. drop the box, spot the box.

bogies: the entire rear end assembly of a tandem-axle tractor.
Cf. dead axle, drivers, joe dog, pig, pusher, powered by rubber bands, spider, twin screw.

boll weevil: a novice truck driver.

Cf. aviator, cog stripper, cowboy, eight-miler, hoo-hooer, real amateur, Sears-Roebuck license, sheep herder, tailgating.

bone crusher: a rough-riding truck, usually a cab-over because of the location of the steering axle beneath the driver's compartment.

Syn.: kidney buster.

Cf. air ride.

bonnet: **1.** the protective covering over the air intake that keeps water or other alien substances from entering the air system.

Cf. bird feeder, breather.

2. the hood on any long-nose tractor.

Cf. whalenose.

boomer: a heavy-weight metal device composed of two hooks linked to a short lever. Used with long chains, they serve to tie down a load on a flat bed or lowboy trailer. "Boomer" is the correct form of the word binder. Originally used by loggers, the form "binder" arose because a boomer binds things together.

Syn.: binder.

Cf. boom it down, button her up, chains and binders, cheater bar, tarp.

boom it down: to secure the chains and binders on a flat bed or lowboy trailer.

Cf. boomer, chains and binders, swede.

boom wagon: a truck carrying explosives.

Cf. dangerous articles, red label load, suicide jockey, widow-maker.

boondockin': the truckers' practice of avoiding all major roads, of traveling on less frequented ones, when running illegally.

Cf. back-pasture hauler, four-laner, hot load, Moonlight Express, runnin' hot, wildcatter.

boss her: to back a trailer into position, usually at a dock or loading platform.

Cf. jacking it around, look-see window, spot the box.

both axles pulling: refers to the action of a full or twin screw rig.

Syn.: two axles pulling.

Cf. bogies, dead axle, double-axle, tandem drive.

bottom dumps: the bottom gates in a trailer through which it is unloaded.

Cf. bathtub dump, hopper body, side dumps, tipper.

Botts Dots: nicknamed by truckers for one of the inventors, these are raised reflective pavement markers that are being increasingly used on highways to replace painted white lines. They cut down on accidents, are easier to see in bad weather, reduce lane changing, and save drivers' nerves. They were first used in California.

box: **1.** the semi-trailer, or body, of a truck.

Syn.: body, semi, tandem.

2. the large, rectangular variety of trailer, as opposed to a flat deck, tanker or pole trailer.

Syn.: van.

Cf. corrugated, rib-side, smooth-side.

brain bag: any briefcase, portfolio or attaché case in which a trucker carries trip reports, company papers, bills of lading, state permits, fuel and expense records, regulations books and any materials of similar nature.

Cf. bible.

brake it off: to slow down the speed of a truck.
Syn.: brakin' 'er down.
Cf. fannin' the brakes, shadow the brake.

brakin' 'er down: slowing down a tractor-trailer.
Syn.: brake it off.
Cf. back off, fannin' the brakes, set her down, shadow the brake, spike it.

breakaway valve: the tractor valve that automatically closes in the event of a broken air line to the trailer, thus conserving the remaining air in the tractor's air system. The breakaway valve is used in the event of a hose break, in hooking up to a trailer, and in dropping a trailer and traveling bobtail.
Syn.: tractor-protection valve.
Cf. charge the trailer, four-way relay emergency valve, set up.

break the unit: to uncouple the tractor from the trailer.
Syn.: drop the box.
Cf. drop it on the nose, pull the pin, spot the body.

breather: the air-intake pipe on a tractor that supplies the engine with air for combustion.
Syn.: bird feeder.
Cf. bonnet, Redwood Tree.

bridge: the distance between one axle and another, or between two sets of axles. Used in some states to ascertain the permissible gross weight for the vehicle.
Cf. axle forward, bridge formula, West Coast rig.

bridge formula: a pattern or set of limitations

used in some states in determining the maximum allowable gross weight for vehicles passing through the state. The factors taken into consideration are the number of axles, the distance between the axles, the overall length of the vehicle, and the gross combination weight of the truck.

Cf. stretch out.

broker: **1.** an owner-operator leased to a company.

Cf. company man, trip lease, wildcatter.

2. a fleet owner who has sublet his rigs to another company.

3. an independent agent who finds loads for a company.

broke to lead: said of a truck that has to be towed to a garage or repair shop.

Cf. cut her water off and read her meter, rehaul.

brownie: a three-speed auxiliary gearbox, the speeds being low-split, direct or intermediate, and high-split or overdrive, the highest speed in the box. Originally built in 1936 by the Brownolite Transmission Co., the originators of the auxiliary gear box, the brownie was first manufactured for use in Mormon Harrison fire trucks to increase their pick-up speed.

Cf. aux box, gearboxes, two-stick transmission.

brownie points: theoretical points gained by a trucker who goes out of his way to do a favor for a dispatcher. Such a driver would be spoken of disparagingly by his fellows if they uncovered the act.

Cf. bid run, connivin' canary, dispatcher, flying orders, gravy hauler, milk run, roster.

bubble burner: a gas rig that runs on propane gas.
Cf. juice jockey, oil burner, percolator, smoker.

bubble gum machine: the flashing light on the roof of a highway patrol car.
Syn.: gumball machine.
Cf. big hat, bird dog, cop caller, cop spotters.

bubble-nose White: a small cabover tractor manufactured by White Motors whose front profile is rounded.
Cf. Mexican Freightliner, rinky dink.

bucket: an engine cylinder.
Cf. banger, four-lunger.

bucket of bolts: a dilapidated truck; one that rattles while being driven. May be used derogatorily or affectionately in reference to a truck in sound condition.
Syn.: crate, dog, gunny sack job, junker.
Cf. been around the Horn, residenter.

buckhorn pipes: twin smokestacks that have a pronounced curve at the top so that the exhaust exits to the side instead of straight up into the air.
Syn.: goathorns.
Cf. bark, gutted, smitty, smokestack, spittoon muffler, twin chimneys, woodpecker.

Budd wheels: wheels that have a solid rather than a spoke center and are bolted fast to the hub. They have five, six, eight or ten holes around the periphery.
Cf. babymoon hubcaps, square wheels.

build a fire: **1**. to run a rig at or near top speed; the smokestack is probably throwing a flame, too.
Syn.: gettin' it done, haul the mail, pour on the coals, tacked out, top off.
2. to start and warm up a cold engine,
Syn.: fire it up, kick 'er over, shake down the ashes, wind 'er up.

bulk freight: freight not in packages or containers.
Cf. bill of lading, L.T.L., minnie.

bulkhead: the shield at the front of a flat deck or single-drop trailer that prevents the load from shifting forward and striking the rear of the cab.
Syn.: header board.
Cf. glad hand, headache rack, nose.

bull dog: a tractor manufactured by Mack.
Cf. follow the bulldog.

bullet lights: large, chrome, bullet-shaped clearance lights on a tractor. They are a luxury option sometimes added to a tractor to improve its appearance.
Syn.: bus markers, torpedoes.
Cf. clearance lights.

bull hauler: a driver who hauls cattle. Other truckers often refer derogatorily to bull haulers as hog haulers because the difference in smell is slight.
Syn.: grunt-and-squeal jockey, shoat and goat conductor.
Cf. bull rack, cackle crate, Pork Chop Express, possum belly.

bull nose: the part of the van body used by a

household goods mover that extends forward over part of the cab. It is so designed to increase the storage space in the van.

Cf. bedbug hauler.

bull rack: a livestock trailer.

Syn.: pullman, shoat boat.

Cf. bull hauler, possum belly.

bumble bee: a two-cycle engine.

Cf. four-banger, six-banger.

bumper signs: it is customary among truckers to paint a slogan, name or nickname on the tractor, usually on the bumper. Most bumper signs fall into one of five categories: **(1)** a name, of the trucker, his wife, his sweetheart, his children or the tractor itself; **(2)** a name of a song; **(3)** a colloquial slogan; (4) a humorous description of the driver; **(5)** a reference to the driver's amatory ability.

The following list is a representative selection of the bumper signs seen on tractors.

Road Runner
Old Ironsides
Thunder Road
'Jamer Wagon
(Pajama Wagon)
International Hotel
Papa's Playpen
Mother's Worry
Gofer Broke
Miss Behavin'
Big Daddy's Back in Town
Wrinkle Dink
Flying Stud
Tasmanian Devil
Sin or Walk
Miss Manookie
Home Breaker
Too Little to Smoke
John 13:16
Ricky Shay
Hillbilly
Born Toulouse
Widow-Maker
Day Late & a Dollar Short
Wheels of Taxation
God is My Copilot

Little Emery's Dad
Old Smoothie
Chevy Chaser
Old Bess
Smoker
Slo-mo-tion
Tennessee Walker
Jolly Green Giant
Noah's Ark
Mayflower
Rapid Rickshaw
Dragon Wagon
New York Belle
Mighty Me
Jo-Jo Yo-Yo
Miss Take
Dixie Pride
Don't Cry Girls, I'll Be Back
Big Daddy's Movin' On
Blue Angel
Rebel
Road Fever
Charlie Brown
Phantom 309
How Sweet It Is
Here Come de Judge
Sweet Thing

bundle buggy: a delivery truck.
Syn.: candy wagon, city flyer, puddle jumper.
Cf. tap dancer.

bunk: the sleeping area in a tractor.
Cf. sleeper, sleeper cab, suicide box.

bunker: the compartment for ice in a reefer.
Cf. cold blow, ice man, putt-putt, reefer.

burn the breeze: to drive at high speed.
Syn.: barrel on down the road, run wide open, smokin' in high gear.
Cf. dig out, hook 'er into high.

burn up the road: to drive fast.
Syn.: big hole it, burn up the rubber, highball it.

burn up the rubber: to drive at or near top speed.
Syn.: burn up the road, pour on the coals.

bus markers: large clearance lights.
Syn.: torpedoes, bullet lights.
Cf. marker lights, use the feelers.

butterfly: a hinged covering over the open end of

a tractor's exhaust pipe. It keeps water from entering the stack when the rig is not in use, but when the truck is running the butterfly opens because of pressure from the exhaust.
Syn.: Bob White, woodpecker.
Cf. butterfly valve, flame thrower, gutted, smitty, spittoon muffler, twin chimneys.

butterfly valve: **1.** the exhaust covering valve in the exhaust manifold that retards exhaust and heat to cause back pressure and to heat the engine. **2.** a part of an exhaust-type Jake brake.
Cf. butterfly, Jake brake, shutters.

butt kit: an ashtray in a tractor.
Cf. dog box, stove and fiddle, saddle.

button her up: to tie down the load on a semi-trailer; especially, to tie down the tarpaulin on a flat bed or rag top trailer.
Cf. boom it down, chains and binders, load her heavy on the high side, open top, sunshine tarps.

buy up an orchard: to have an accident by running off the side of the road into the brush or trees.
Cf. belly up, berm, between the fence rows, pile up, spin out, total it out.

C

cab: **1.** the driver's compartment of the tractor. **2.** generally speaking, the tractor itself.
Cf. cabover, conventional cab.

cab control levers: levers in a tractor cab that control the power takeoff and the hydraulic hoist, if the tractor is so equipped.

cab forward: a tractor whose design places the driver well forward; the cab is over or in front of the steering axle.
Cf. axle forward, axle back.

cabover: a tractor with the engine located below the driver's compartment. The tractor has a straight profile, as opposed to that of a conventional cab, which has a forward projection or nose. The two advantages of cabovers are that they are easier to steer in tight spots or small docking areas and that they have a shorter wheelbase, which means that they can haul a longer semi-trailer and consequently a greater pay load.
Syn.: blunt-nose, cab-over-engine, flat face, pug, snub-nose.
Cf. cherry picker, kidney buster, tilt cab.

cab-over-engine: a tractor on which the cab is located above the engine.
Syn.: cabover, C.O.E., snub-nose.
Cf. conventional cab.

cackle crate: a truck hauling live poultry. Chicken crates are usually stacked on a flat bed trailer.
Cf. Pork Chop Express, shoat and goat conductor, shoat boat, weeder geese hauler.

C.A.E.: a tractor in which the **c**ab is located **a**longside the **e**ngine.
Cf. C.B.E., C.O.E., half cab.

California air: the extra air tank on a truck equipped with three air tanks instead of two.

A safety precaution, the third tank is used as a reserve to release the emergency brake, which goes on automatically if the truck loses air from the first two tanks. This reserve allows the trucker to pull off the road away from other vehicles. It is so named because California's regulations require a truck to be equipped with a third air tank the second time it enters the state and every time thereafter.

Cf. emerjensen, Jake brake, mag brake, sucker brake, West Coast hookup.

California tires: tires with little or no tread remaining.

Syn.: cheater slicks, racin' slicks, rags.

Cf. duals, pumpkin, rider, skins.

camelback: a tractor equipped with a dromedary box for storing extra freight; the fifth wheel is located to the rear of the box.

Cf. drom box.

candles: flares; generally used in emergency situations to mark off the scene of an accident or to warn oncoming motorists of a broken-down vehicle in the road or on the shoulder.

Cf. pots.

candy wagon: a lightweight truck.

Syn.: leapin' Lena, puddle jumper.

Cf. bundle buggy, straight job.

can the motor: to run the motor at high speed while in a low gear.

Syn.: overspeed.

Cf. gun the motor, lugging, tack.

cant hook: a long pole with a spiked end and a

steel hook used to turn logs by loggers and by truckers who drive logging rigs.
Syn.: muley cow.

cap: a tire recap of only the road-surface area.
Cf. full cap, surface cap.

cardboard driver: a new driver going through a trial period with a trucking company; so named because the tractor he owns and drives carries cardboard signs instead of the permanent decals affixed by the company.
Cf. decals, pretties, pull one's decals.

carrier: a person or company that provides transportation service as a business.
Cf. common carrier, contract carrier, exempt carrier, for-hire carrier, private carrier, specialized carrier.

car transporter: a specially adapted tractor-trailer unit designed for the transportation of cars or pickup trucks. It accommodates from six to eight cars on the double-decker racks and is usually pulled by a conventional cab for reasons of saving space.
Cf. trailer types.

cat: short for a Caterpillar engine in a tractor.

cat's eyes: the reflective markers on slender posts that mark the edge of a highway.
Cf. Botts Dots, spooks.

cattle light: a spotlight mounted on the cab used to help the driver find livestock on the open range.
Syn.: horse light, house number hunters, name plate finders.
Cf. coon light, ditch light.

C.B.E.: a tractor on which the **c**ab is located **be**hind the **e**ngine: a conventional cab.

Cf. C.A.E., C.O.E., cab forward.

cement mixer: a truck with a noisy engine or transmission.

Cf. singer.

centipede: a multiaxle tractor-trailer combination; one with so many sets of tires that it resembles a huge centipede.

Cf. Michigan rig, rolling doughnuts, semi and pup, train.

chain-drive pocketbook: a folded leather wallet fastened to a trucker's belt by a thin chain.

Syn.: chain-drive wallet.

Cf. double-clutchin' boots, fifty-mission cap, singer, two-speed gloves.

chain-drive wallet: a wallet carried in a trucker's back pocket and fastened to his belt by means of a small chain.

Syn.: chain-drive pocketbook.

Cf. split-shiftin' gloves.

chains and binders: the securing devices and chains used to tie down the load on a flat bed or lowboy trailer.

Cf. button her up, boomer, clamp on the binders, suicide coil, swede, tarps.

charge a trailer: to flip the switch (tractor protection valve) in the tractor that builds up the air in the air reservoir or supply tank of the trailer for operating the trailer's brakes. When a trucker unhooks from a trailer, he flips the switch back the other way to keep the air from escaping through the glad hands on the air hoses.

Cf. air hose, blow him up, four-way relay emergency valve, glad hand, tractor-protection valve.

chaser: **1.** a company employee who hurries the loading and unloading of trucks at a dock.
Syn.: pusher.
Cf. checker.
2. a garage employee who "chases down" parts needed for truck repairs.

cheater axle: an extra axle that bears on the ground only when the truck is loaded. A rig so equipped can save on turnpike tolls based on axle weight when it is deadheading or only lightly loaded.
Cf. air-lift axle.

cheater bar: any bar used to obtain additional leverage, as in tightening tire lugs or in securing the chains and binders on a load.
Syn.: swede.
Cf. boom it down.

cheater boards: a side board used on a dump trailer to raise the sides and increase the carrying capacity. The carrying capacity of dump and gravel trailers is usually measured in a "water-level hauling capacity"; because water cannot be heaped up as gravel can, this is considered a true measure of capacity.
Syn.: hungry boards, side boards.
Cf. struck capacity.

cheater slicks: tires with the tread worn off.
Syn.: California tires, racin' slicks, rags.
Cf. baloneys, duals, dusting, micks, pumpkin, rider, skins.

checker: an employee hired by a company to de-

tect irregularities in the drivers' over-the-road activities.
Syn.: spotter.
Cf. chaser.

cherry picker: an extremely high cabover tractor. Originally the term referred specifically to the old-time cabover model Mack tractor, one of the tallest cabovers ever manufactured.
Syn.: peach picker.

Chi: Chicago.
Cf. Bean Town, Big Town, Frisco, L.A.

chief hood lifter: garage superintendent.
Cf. grease monkey, ice man, maniac, sledgehammer mechanic.

chimney sweep run: a truck run that involves extensive freight handling by the trucker or the handling of dirty freight.
Cf. clock load, fingerprint, flyer, peddle run, pension run, white collar man.

chock the wheels: to place wedges or blocks of metal or wood in front of and behind the wheels of a tractor-trailer when parking it to keep the rig from rolling in the event of parking brake failure.
Cf. shut 'er down.

choke and puke: a run-down truck stop.
Syn.: greasy spoon, heartburn palace, pigpen.
Cf. fuel stop, pig, truck stop.

chop a turn: to cut a corner.
Syn.: bite a turn.
Cf. need a hinge, split-arc, wrap 'er around the bend.

Christmas tree: a truck with many extra clearance

lights; some drivers even put their own or their company's initials on the rig. Other truckers refer to the rig as "Bein' lit up like a Christmas tree."

Syn.: rolling lighthouse.

Cf. identification lights, idiot light, torpedoes.

church key: an oil can opener.

Cf. granny rag.

cinchers: the brakes of a truck.

Syn.: anchors, binders.

Cf. emerjensen, hot shoe, jack-off bar, sucker brake.

circus wagon: a low-sided trailer with metal bows over the top that support a tarpaulin cover.

Syn.: rag top.

Cf. open top.

city flyer: a short trailer used for making deliveries in a city.

Cf. shag, straight job.

claim: a demand for payment to compensate for freight damage that is supposed to have occurred while the cargo was in the hands of the carrier.

Cf. bill of lading, minnie, overage, shortage, shovel.

clamp on the binders: **1.** to apply the brakes.

Syn.: reach for the air, throw out the anchor.

Cf. brakin' 'er down, dynamite the brakes.

2. to tighten the chains and binders holding the load on a lowboy or flat bed trailer.

Cf. boomer, button her up.

clean bore: refers to a tanker trailer without interior compartments.

Cf. baffle.

clean his clock: to pass another vehicle, especially another tractor-trailer, with great speed.
Syn.: dust 'em off, smoke him.
Cf. big hole it, build a fire, haul the mail, tacked out.

clearance lights: the small lights that outline a truck's length and breadth at night or in bad weather. The lamps at the front and sides are amber; those visible from the rear are red. The Interstate Commerce Commission has set up standards regulating their size, manufacture, location and manner of attachment to the tractor-trailer unit.
Syn.: marker lights, running lights.
Cf. bullet lights, bus markers, identification lights, rolling lighthouse, torpedoes.

clock load: a shipment whose departure from the consignor and arrival at its destination are punched in and out on a time clock. The driver is thus under a good deal of pressure to make delivery as quickly as he can.
Cf. chimney sweep run, flyer, hot load, red label load, runnin' hot.

close the gates: to close the rear doors on a trailer.
Cf. tailgate it.

club: an old, beat-up trailer.
Syn.: sled.
Cf. been around the Horn, crate, drag, junker, sagamore.

clunker: any old tractor, rolling junk.
Syn.: bucket of bolts, crate, gunny sack job, junker.

Cf. been around the Horn.

clutch artist: **1.** a trucker who can shift any type of transmission without raking gears or losing engine revolutions per minute. **2.** generally speaking, any truck driver.

Syn.: commercial tourist, distribution technician, double-clutchin' man, gear shifter, semi driver, spinner.

coach: a mobile home in transit to a dealer or a home site.

Cf. shanty shaker, stairstep.

C.O.E.: a cabover, or **c**ab-**o**ver-**e**ngine tractor, in which the driver's compartment is located over the engine. When viewed from the side, the tractor has a straight profile without the frontal projection of a conventional cab. Truckers have nicknamed these cabs "snub-nose," "blunt-nose" and "pug" because of their appearance.

Cf. cab forward, conventional cab, tilt cab.

coffee pot: a restaurant, especially one that caters to truck drivers.

Cf. choke and puke, fuel stop, heartburn palace, truck stop.

coffin box: a sleeper added onto a conventional cab.

Syn.: suicide box.

Cf. slumber slot, pajama wagon.

cog stripper: a trucker who shifts gears noisily.

Cf. clutch artist, split the cogs, scratch one in.

cold blow: air conditioning.

Cf. bunker, putt-putt, reefer.

cold box: a trailer with a refrigeration unit for the transportation of perishables.

Syn.: ice box, reefer.

Cf. bunker, cold blow, dry box, ice man, putt-putt, railer.

combinations: tractor-trailers are often referred to by the number of their axles: a three-axle combination is a single-axle tractor and a single-axle trailer; a four-axle job is a single-axle tractor and a tandem-axle trailer; a five-axle rig is a single-axle tractor and a triaxle trailer or a tandem tractor and a tandem trailer; a six-axle combination is a tandem-axle tractor and a triaxle trailer.

Cf. Michigan rig, single axle, semi and pup, tandem, triples.

commercial highway engineer: a truck driver.

Syn.: distribution technician, gear jammer, spinner.

Cf. trucker, relocation consultant.

commercial tourist: a trucker.

Syn.: double-clutchin' man, spinner.

commodity: any goods or articles that a trucking company transports. Some commodities are exempt; that is, they may be transported without the requisite operating authority of a common or contract hauler.

Cf. carrier.

common carrier: a trucking company that hauls goods for anyone who has the money, as opposed to a contract or a private carrier. Rates and routes for most common carriers are I.C.C. regulated, but common carriers that have irregular routes are not regulated by any government agency.

Cf. exempt carrier, for-hire carrier, grandfather rights, Moonlight Express.

company man: 1. a trucker employed by a company and who drives a company truck.
Cf. owner-operator.
2. used in a derogatory sense, "company man" may mean a squealer, a man who places his loyalty to the company above his loyalty to his fellow drivers.

concentrator: the trucker of a two-man operation who happens to be behind the wheel at a given moment.
Cf. navigator.

connecting carrier: a carrier that interchanges trailers with another company in order to deliver shipments to destinations beyond its own operating authority but within that of the second carrier.
Cf. interline.

connivin' canary: a woman trucker who uses her wits and resources to the fullest extent to obtain good loads.
Cf. brownie points, dispatcher, gravy hauler.

containerization: in national and international scale transportation, the growing tendency to treat a trailer as one large package of goods to be shipped to a specific destination, thus eliminating the loading and unloading of the trailer customary in "part-load" shipments.
Cf. birdyback, fishyback, L.T.L., minnie, piggyback.

contract carrier: a trucking company not licensed for public hire that contracts to haul goods exclusively for a specific company or for a limited number of companies.
Cf. carrier, for-hire carrier, private carrier.

conventional cab: a tractor with the engine located in front of the driver's compartment; it has a frontal projection, or "nose," when viewed from the side. The advantages of a conventional cab are **(1)** as smoother ride, **(2)** the driver is somewhat protected, in case of head-on accident, by the engine, and **(3)** the driver has to cope with fewer blind spots because he is closer to the road.
Syn.: C.B.E.
Cf. axle back, axle forward, C.A.E., C.O.E.

conversion hoist: a hoist on a straight job that is designed to change flat bed bodies into dumping bodies.

converter dolly: the coupling device composed of one or two axles and a fifth wheel by which a semi-trailer can be coupled to the rear of a tractor-trailer combination, forming a double bottom rig.
Syn.: dollies, double hookup, jo-jo, whippletree.
Cf. full trailer, kite without a tail.

convertible: a flat bed trailer that can be used either as a flat or as a high sides trailer by the removal or the addition of side panels.
Syn.: converto-van.
Cf. open top, platform, set of racks.

converto-van: a trailer that converts into a flat bed or a van by means of removable sides and head board.
Syn.: convertible.
Cf. open top, set of racks.

convoy: **1.** a group of trucks from the same company that runs together from the same shipper to the same destination. **2.** several trucks running together in a group down a highway.
Syn.: rat race.
Cf. family reunion.

coon light: **1.** a spotlight aimed at the right edge of the road.
Syn.: ditch light.
2. an out-of-adjustment headlight on a car or truck.

cop caller: **1.** a truck with squealing brakes.
Cf. big hat.
2. a recapped tire with an unbroken tread line that creates an exceptional amount of road noise.
Syn.: Pennsylvania caps.
Cf. full cap, singers, singing, surface cap.

copilot: a second driver on a long haul.
Syn.: second driver, shotgun, swamper.
Cf. concentrator, divorced, lead driver, married, navigator, roving team.

copilots: stay-awake pills, the use of which is discouraged by the I.C.C., the trucking industry, and truck-line officials.
Syn.: helpers, Upjohns.
Cf. bennie, L.A. turnaround.

cop spotter: a rearview mirror.
Cf. peek-a-boo mirror, Volkswagen spotter, West Coast mirror.

corn binder: any tractor manufactured by International Harvester.

Cf. Bifocal International, Emeryville, In Hock Constantly, spaceship, two-story Emeryville, West Coast binder.

corrugated: said of a semi-trailer whose side ridges run horizontally to the ground.

Cf. rib-side, smooth-side.

cowboy: **1.** a reckless driver, a phenomenon among truckers, who as professionals are the safest drivers on the road. **2.** an affectionate form of address among truckers.

Cf. aviator, boll weevil, sheep herder, tail-board artist, truck jockey.

cowpath: a narrow, two-lane blacktop road.

Cf. berm, four-laner, line, pike, religious road.

crackerbox Jimmy: the old-time cabover model tractor manufactured by General Motors Corporation; so named because of its elongated rectangular appearance. The cab resembled a crackerbox stood on end.

Syn.: matchbox Jimmy.

Cf. Detroit Diesel, Hillbilly Special, Jamie, screamin' Lena.

crank: a truck's starter.

Cf. armstrong starter, gesundheit starter, kick 'er over, stew winder, wind 'er up.

crankshaft: a shaft in the engine that converts the reciprocating motion of the cylinders to the rotary motion of the drive shaft.

crate: **1.** a tractor-trailer that is old and dilapidated.

Syn.: bucket of bolts, clunker, gunny sack job, residenter.

2. used derogatorily, any tractor-trailer or rig.

crate of sand: a cargo of sugar.
Syn.: load of sand.
Cf. load of suds, load of wind, red label load, smoker.

creeper gear: the lowest gear or the lowest combination of gears a tractor has. Usually used when starting from a complete stop, for extra power, or for climbing steep hills.
Syn.: grandma gear, number-one hole.
Cf. pay hole, wobbly hole.

cube: short for cubic feet, the measure of a trailer's carrying capacity.
Cf. drop bottom, high cube.

cup and saucer: a device used on logging rigs that, like the fifth wheel, allows the rig to turn. The log bunk center (cup) performs a pivoting action in the saucer when the rig is turned.
Cf. inverted fifth wheel, removable kingpin.

curb weight: the weight of an empty tractor-trailer minus driver and cargo but including fuel, oil and all standard equipment.
Cf. G.C.W., G.V.W.

cut back: said of any tractor engine whose governor has been turned down or whose fuel proportion in the fuel-to-air ratio has been decreased.
Syn.: weaned out.
Cf. cut 'er down, open 'er up, turn the wick up.

cut 'er down: **1.** to turn the governor down in order to decrease the engine's RPM. **2.** to decrease the fuel portion in relation to the amount of air being burned in the cylinders.
Syn.: weaned out.

Cf. set it up, turn the wick up.

cut her water off and read her meter: to stop a truck and look for engine or tire trouble.

Cf. broke to lead, rehaul.

D

Dago: San Diego, California.

Cf. Big Town, Frisco, L.A.

dangerous articles: a classification of commodities transported by truck that includes explosives, flammables, compressed gas, oxidizing materials, poisons, corrosives and radioactive materials. These articles require special consideration in handling and shipping and are subject to stringent I.C.C. regulations.

Cf. boom wagon, red label load, suicide jockey, widow-maker.

dangle the cat: to drive a truck with an engine manufactured by Caterpillar.

Cf. cat.

day cab: a tractor that has no sleeping compartment.

Syn.: straight.

Cf. pajama wagon, suicide box.

Dayton wheels: spoke wheels on a tractor.

Syn.: manure spreader wheels, square wheels, wobblers.

Cf. babymoon hubcaps, Budd wheels.

dead axle: an axle that serves only to raise the weight of cargo a tractor-trailer can haul; it has no pulling power.

Cf. drivers, live axle, pusher, spider, tag axle, twin screw.

deadhead: to run empty.
Syn.: hauling postholes.
Cf. bobtail miles, deadhead haul.

deadhead haul: a run in which a trucker travels to or from a destination without a cargo or payload.
Syn.: load of postholes.
Cf. bobtail miles, zephyr haul.

Death on Truckers: truckese for the Department of Transportation (D.O.T.).
Cf. I-Can-Catch, I-men, P.U.C.

decals: plastic signs glued onto, or otherwise affixed to, the doors of a tractor. Decals bear the name of the trucking line, the city and state of the home terminal, and the I.C.C. and P.U.C. numbers for the various states in which the carrier has authority to operate.
Cf. cardboard driver, pretties, pull one's decals.

deck: (noun) the top surface of a trailer, the part on which the cargo rests.
Cf. flat deck, step-deck trailer.
(verb) to place one trailer on top of a second to transfer them simultaneously to another locale.
Syn.: double deck.
Cf. triple deck.

deck and four-wheeler: a semi-trailer pulling a pup trailer.
Syn.: semi and pup.
Cf. kite without a tail.

decked out: said of a tractor with a special paint job and fancy accessories.
Syn.: all dolled up.
Cf. floating chrome, hillbilly chrome, rolling palace, zebra stripes.

dedicated: a tractor-trailer combination or a trailer is said to be dedicated to a particular terminal if it must return there directly after making a delivery in order to pick up another load.
Cf. flyer, flying orders, peddle run, turn.

deep-reduction valve: part of the fifteen-speed Roadranger transmission, it is used only under adverse conditions: in off-highway operations, in deep sand or in mud, and when getting a heavily loaded truck underway.
Cf. Roadranger, searcher, splitter.

defrostos: a type of West Coast mirror with a heating element used to keep the mirror from frosting over in cold climates.
Cf. cop spotters, Volkswagen spotters, West Coast mirrors.

delayed: used humorously, a truck driver never becomes lost but he may sometimes be delayed.

detachable gooseneck: the gooseneck on a lowboy trailer is removable on certain models to make it easier to load the trailer. It is designed so that, when the trucker drives the tractor away from the parked lowboy, the gooseneck of the trailer remains attached to the fifth wheel. The cargo is then loaded onto the lowered front end of the trailer.

Cf. expandable lowboy, outriggers, lowboy, well.

Detroit Diesel: the market name for engines manufactured by General Motors Corporation but intended for placement in tractors of other makes.

Syn.: screamin' Lena.

Cf. billy goat, crackerbox Jimmy, **G**arage **M**an's **C**ompanion, Hillbilly Special.

Detroit vibrator: a Chevrolet tractor.

Syn.: Texas Autocar, Texas KW.

diapers: a winter front on a tractor; anything used to cover the radiator or front of a truck to keep cold air from entering in the winter and to conserve warmth from the engine.

Syn.: bandaids.

Cf. bandaged up, eskimo, pneumonia sedan, winter front.

diesel: **1.** a type of internal combustion engine invented by Rudolf Diesel, a German engineer (1858–1913). It differs from the gasoline engine in that it uses compression to raise air temperature to the igniting point, while the gasoline engine is spark-ignited. **2.** generally speaking, any tractor with a diesel engine.

Syn.: smoker.

Cf. banger, bubble burner, juice jockey, oil burner.

differential lock: found only on full or twin-screw tractors, this valve can be set at "lock" to lock both rear axles together so that they pull as one for off-the-road operation (only). The differential lock is never used for over-the-road operation because the rear end assembly of the drive axles could be ruined if the tractor hit a bad bump.

Cf. drive axle, rear end assembly, twin screw.

dig out: to make a fast start.

Syn.: peel out.

Cf. barrel on down the road, haul the mail, running start.

direct: **1.** any gear in which the main shaft and the countershaft of the transmission turn as one unit. **2.** the intermediate gradient in a three-speed auxiliary gear box.

Cf. high side, low side, over and under, overdrive.

Dirge: a Dodge tractor.

dispatch: the department in a trucking company that decides which driver receives what driving assignment.

Cf. bid run, roster, roving team.

dispatcher: the man who works a company's dispatch; he is responsible for matching the available drivers with the loads to be covered and for assigning the latter to the men when they call in after making a delivery. The dispatcher's lot is a difficult one: either he keeps the management satisfied, to the disgruntlement of the drivers, or he keeps the drivers happy, to the dissatisfaction of the managing powers.

Cf. brownie points, flying orders.

distribution technician: a truck driver.

Syn.: commercial highway engineer, clutch artist, double-clutchin' man, gear shifter, semidriver.

Cf. trucker.

ditch light: a spotlight directed toward the right side of the road; it is usually mounted on the upper front corner of the tractor.
Syn.: coon light.
Cf. nameplate finders.

division: a group of drivers working for one company and located (home town or home terminal) in a certain area of the country.

divorced: refers to the separation of the members of a two-man operation.
Cf. married, run double.

dock: a platform at which trucks load and unload.
Cf. chaser, dock walloper, swamper.

dock it: to park a truck at a dock.
Cf. shagging, spotter, yard mule.

dock monkey: a helper who assists the loading and unloading of trucks at a dock, and the movement of freight from one part of a dock to another.
Syn.: dock walloper.

dock walloper: a helper who loads and unloads trailers.
Syn.: dock monkey, swamper.
Cf. fork lift.

dog: a truck with little power or a poor appearance.
Syn.: bucket of bolts, crate, gutless wonder, sick horse.

dog box: the high covering over the engine in the center of the driver's area of a cabover. Usually table height, it may have placed upon it some of the gauges of the instrument panel, a radio, the glove compartment, a stereo unit, an ashtray or other accessories.
Syn.: dog house.

dog catcher: **1**. any rig fast enough to catch up to and pass a Greyhound bus, and therefore a title of high honor. **2**. any fast truck.
Cf. flagship, Hound.

dog house: the covering over the engine in the center of the driver's compartment of a cab-over.
Syn.: dog box.
Cf. fire wall.

dog leg: a type of intersection characteristic of New Jersey roads that is formed by a lane from the right-hand side of the road that curves away from the highway and then crosses it at right angles. A dog leg enables traffic to make a left-hand lane of traffic on the highway. It derives its name from its appearance when viewed from above.
Syn.: jughandle.
Cf. berm, holy road, line, spooks.

doglegging: a condition in which one of the cross-members of the tractor frame has failed to keep the entire frame square, with the result that one side rail advances. The rear tractor wheels do not track the front wheels, as they should, but follow off to the side. This is a serious situation because the alignment of the drive-shaft components is disturbed and the tires and bearings are subjected to additional wear.
Syn.: dog track, dog trot.

dog track: to not run true; said of a truck or semi-trailer that does not track correctly.
Syn.: dog trot, doglegging.

dog trot: to track incorrectly; said of a truck or a trailer; named for the action of a trotting dog.
Syn.: dog track, doglegging.

dollies: **1.** the coupling device composed of one or two axles and a fifth wheel by which a semitrailer can be coupled to the rear of a tractor-trailer unit, making the combination into a double-bottom rig.
Syn.: converter dolly, double hookup, jo-jo, whippletree.
2. the supporting gear that holds up the front end of a trailer when it is parked without the tractor.
Syn.: landing gear.
Cf. drop it on the nose, drop the box.

dolly: a small platform mounted on wheels that is used in a warehouse to move freight.
Cf. dock walloper, doodle-bug.

donkey wheels: an extra set of wheels, to the rear of the drivers on a straight job, that rests on the ground only when the vehicle is loaded.
Syn.: pony wheels.
Cf. cheater axle.

doodle-bug: a small tractor used to pull two-axle dollies in a warehouse.
Cf. dolly, spotter, yard mule.

double-axle: **1.** a tractor with two rear axles.
Syn.: tandem.
Cf. bogies, twin screw.
2. a tandem-axle trailer.
Syn.: tandem.
Cf. single axle, triaxle.

double-bottom rig: a rig composed of a tractor, a semi-trailer, converter dollies and a second trailer.
Syn.: doubles, twin trailers, set of joints.
Cf. deck and four-wheeler, dual shorts, long double, Michigan rig, rollin' doughnuts, short bottom, trainman's license, triples, truck-trailer.

double-clutching: the technique by which a driver shifts gears without clashing them by pumping the clutch twice.

The reason for double-clutching is that the transmission turns over faster than the engine; when a driver double-clutches, the engine speed falls off and slows the transmission.
Cf. double-clutchin' boots, kick 'em.

double-clutchin' boots: a trucker's boots; so named because of the technique of double-clutching.
Cf. chain-drive wallet, fifty-mission cap, split-shiftin' gloves.

double-clutchin' man: a trucker.
Syn.: commercial tourist, gear jammer, line driver, semi driver.

double deck: (noun) a lowboy trailer in which the top surface of the frame has a drop or trough that rises over the rear axles to its former level.
Syn.: double-drop trailer.
Cf. drop frame, single-drop trailer, well.
(verb) to place one trailer on top of another to transport them both to another location.
Cf. deck, triple deck.

double-drop trailer: a lowboy trailer with a drop

or trough in the top surface of the frame. The deck of the trailer is the same height on each side of the drop.
Syn.: double deck.
Cf. single-drop trailer.

double hookup: originally a single-axle dolly, now a coupling device of one or more axles and a fifth wheel used in a double-bottom rig to join the second trailer to the rear of the first.
Syn.: dollies, jo-jo, whippletree.
Cf. semi and pup, tongue, train.

double mount: a type of saddle mount operation in which two tractors are mounted on and transported by a third, as contrasted to a single saddle mount, in which only one additional tractor is mounted on the power unit.
Cf. full mount, saddle mount, triple mount.

double overdrive: the fastest combination of gears in a transmission when each top gear is an overdrive gear. For instance, a transmission composed of a five-speed main box and a three-speed rear axle would have a double overdrive if the top gear in the main box were an overdrive gear.
Cf. aux box, gearboxes, main box, overdrive, two-speed axle, two-way split, three-speed axle, three-way split, triplex.

double reduction: a rear end assembly with two ring gears and one pinion gear. A double-reduction rear lasts three times longer than a single-reduction rear end assembly.
Cf. banjo, pig, rear end assembly.

doubles: a rig composed of a tractor and two trailers.
Syn.: double-bottom rig, set of joints, train, twin trailers.
Cf. centipede, dual shorts, Michigan rig, rolling doughnuts, semi and pup, triples.

douche bag: a container that holds water (and antifreeze solvent in the winter or bug-removing detergent in the summer) to clean the windshields. The windshield washers are manually operated by the driver.

doughnuts: small tires frequently used on drop-bottom trailers to afford greater hauling capacity by lowering the floor level of the box.
Cf. high cube.

down in the corner: refers to the transmission of a truck in low gear; named for the position of the gear sticks when in low.
Syn.: creeper gear, down in the kitchen, grandma gear, growler, ought hole, whistlin' gear.
Cf. whistlin' gear.

down in the kitchen: refers to a truck's transmission in the lowest gear or combination of gears.
Syn.: down in the corner, number-one hole.
Cf. pay hole, wobbly hole.

down time: the time a truck spends in the terminal or repair shop and off the road. Met with as much enthusiasm by truckers as a confrontation with the I.C.C.
Cf. broke to lead, rehaul.

drag: a slow freighter.

Syn.: dog, gutless wonder, sick horse.
Cf. husky oat motor.

drag down: to shift to the lower gears too slowly.
Syn.: lugging.
Cf. drop gears, grab one, kick down, overspeed, tachometer, windmill.

drive axle: as opposed to a dead or tag axle, a drive axle actively pulls the load.
Syn.: drivers, live axle.
Cf. axle, axle weight, bogies, pusher, rear end assembly, spider, tandem drive, twin screw.

drive line: a shaft that connects the transmission to the rear end.
Syn.: drive shaft.
Cf. banjo, crankshaft.

drivers: the drive wheels of a tractor.
Cf. bogies, dead axle, live axle, pusher, twin screw, tandem drive.

drive shaft: a heavy-duty tube that connects the transmission to the rear end assembly of the tractor.
Syn.: drive line.
Cf. crankshaft, pig.

driving lights: lights usually mounted beneath the bumper and used to increase the driver's visibility in poor weather conditions.
Cf. clearance lights, duel spots, torpedoes.

drom box: short for dromedary box.

dromedary box: a metal compartment set on the truck frame behind the cab and ahead of the fifth wheel. As high and wide as a trailer, the dromedary box is about 4½ feet long and serves to increase the cargo capacity of the combination. It is sometimes used as a refrigeration compartment for hauling a small load of perishables in addition to the regular load.

Syn.: drom box.

Cf. camelback.

drop bottom: a trailer whose floor level between the axles is lower than that above the axles. Seen most commonly on livestock trailers and moving vans for reasons of space economy.

Syn.: drop frame.

Cf. high cube, possum belly.

drop-deck flat: a flat bed or flat bottom trailer with a drop in the top surface of the frame. The higher level at the trailer's front end is usually twelve feet long, the drop is one foot in depth, and the lower level is twenty-eight feet long. Overall length is forty feet, as in the standard flat trailer.

Syn.: single-drop trailer, step-deck trailer.

drop frame: a box trailer whose floor level is lower between the axles of the tractor and the axles of the trailer, than it is directly over them.

Syn.: drop bottom.

Cf. possum belly.

drop gears: to down-gear the transmission.

Syn.: kick down, knock it down.

Cf. drag down, grab one, lugging, tachometer.

drop it on the nose: to accidentally pull a tractor away from a parked semi-trailer without first lowering the landing gear of the trailer to support its front end.

Cf. dollies, drop the box, float, nose dive.

drop the box: 1. to unhook the tractor from a trailer, pulling the tractor away and leaving the trailer parked. **2.** more specifically, this refers to dropping a box or van trailer.
Syn.: break the unit, drop the body.
Cf. unlatch.

dry box: a van that does not have a refrigeration unit for the transportation of perishables; used to haul dry freight.
Cf. cold box, ice box, railer, reefer.

dry freight: freight that does not need to be shipped at a specific temperature to prevent spoilage.
Cf. cold box, dry box, feather hauler, reefer.

duals: a pair of wheels and tires mounted together on the same side of one axle.
Cf. barefoot, dusting, pumpkin, rider, singing.

dual shorts: two twenty-foot trailers in a double-bottom rig.
Cf. double-bottom rig, long double, Michigan rig, semi and pup, train.

dual spots: small, round spotlights on a cab, manually controlled by the driver.
Syn.: twin spots.
Cf. horse light, house number hunters, nameplate finders.

dual stacks: two smokestacks, or exhaust pipes, on a tractor.
Syn.: twin chimneys, twin stacks.
Cf. gutted, smitty, spittoon muffler.

dump body: a trailer that can be tilted to unload a cargo of gravel, rocks or sand.
Syn.: tipper.

Cf. bottom dumps, hopper body, wet lines.

duplex: a Mack 10-speed transmission with five gears controlled by a main gearshift and with two gears controlled by an auxiliary gearshift. These two give a high and a low range for each gear, making the total forward speeds ten.

Cf. quadriplex, triplex, two-way split, unishift, two-stick transmission.

dust 'em off: to pass another truck at high speed.

Syn.: clean his clock, smoke him.

Cf. flying low.

dusting: driving with one wheel off the side of the pavement and throwing up a cloud of dust; done purposely by a trucker to discourage a tailgating motorist or traffic cop.

Cf. ride a firebug, rider.

dynamite the brakes: to make an emergency stop.

Syn.: set her down, spike it, throw out the anchor.

E

East Coast hookup: a no longer used brake hookup with separate controlling devices for the brakes on the tractor and on the trailer: the trucker's foot applied the tractor brakes while a hand valve regulated the ones on the trailer. The East Coast hookup was outlawed by the I.C.C. because of the number of jackknife accidents involving rigs with this brake system.

In an emergency, a trucker more often hit the brakes before using the hand control, if he remembered it at all. With the trailer's speed exceeding that of the tractor, the semi would swing sideways into the cab.

Cf. anchors, emerjensen, Johnson bar, monkey bar, West Coast hookup.

eatin' concrete: to drive a truck down a highway.

Cf. grab some gears, push a rig, wheel a rig.

eighteen-wheel rig: a five-axle combination that has eighteen wheels in all (two wheels on the steering axle; four on each of the four other axles).

Syn.: five-axle rig, tandem-tandem.

Cf. eight-wheeler, ten-wheeler.

eight-miler: a careless tourist or trucker who runs down the road with a signal light on for several miles.

Cf. aviator, cog stripper, cowboy, hoo-hooer, lane hopper, real amateur, sheep herder, tail-board artist.

eight-wheeler: short for a four-axle combination, which has eight sets of wheels (the single-axle tractor has four sets; the tandem trailer has four sets).

Cf. combinations, eighteen-wheel rig, six-wheeler, ten-wheeler.

elevator: a hydraulic end gate on a trailer.

Syn.: power lift gate.

eleventh gear: the neutral shift position in a ten-speed transmission; used when the trucker, in driving downhill, throws the transmission out of gear and allows the rig to coast.

Cf. Georgia overdrive, Jewish overdrive, Mexican overdrive, midnight overdrive, thirteenth gear.

emerjensen: the emergency brake.

Syn.: Emma Jesse brake, jack-off bar, Johnson bar.

Cf. anchors, cinchers, trolley-valve handle.

Emeryville: the cabover tractor manufactured by International Harvester in its Emeryville, California, factory.

Syn.: corn binder.

Cf. Bifocal International, four thousand, In Hock Constantly, spaceship.

Emma Jesse brake: truckese for the emergency brake.

Syn.: emerjensen, jack-off bar, Johnson bar.

Cf. hot shoe, Jake brake, trolley-valve handle.

end dump: a trailer that is unloaded by raising the front part to allow the load to slide out the back gate.

Syn.: tipper.

Cf. bottom dumps, dump body.

engine guard: a protective shield mounted beneath the engine.

Syn.: stump jumper.

eskimo: a trucker who drives with the windows wide open in the winter.

Cf. Hunter heater, pneumonia sedan, winter front.

ether: a substance used to start a cold diesel engine in freezing or subfreezing weather.

Cf. ether lock, gumballs, summertime truck.

ether lock: what occurs when too much ether has

been injected into an engine, resulting in a premature diesel combustion that has the effect of "stalemating" the cylinder.

Cf. gumballs, mothballs.

exempt carrier: a company that hauls produce, seafood, raw materials or certain manufactured goods.

Cf. carrier, common carrier, contract carrier, for-hire carrier, private carrier, specialized carrier.

expandable lowboy: a lowboy trailer in which the length of the well can be increased or decreased to suit the requirements of the load.

Cf. pole trailer, stretch flat, stretch lowboy.

express body: an open box truck body on a straight job.

eyeball it: to measure the height, width or length of a trailer's cargo by sight.

Cf. overdimensional load.

eye trouble: the inability to remain awake.

Cf. bedsteader, bennie, roll and rest, pull a sleep job.

F

fair-weather driver: a driver who wheels his rig only in good driving weather. At the first snowflake or icy patch on the road, this trucker pulls into the closest truck stop to weather the "storm."

Syn.: sunshine driver.

Cf. windshield wiper-itis.

fairyland: any roadside park.

family reunion: several trucks from the same company that meet at one truck stop.
Cf. convoy.

fannin' the brakes: alternately applying and releasing the brakes when descending a long hill with the rig geared down; done as the engine reaches its maximum revolutions per minute in order to keep the truck from picking up too much speed.
Cf. back off, brakin' 'er down, windmill.

feather: to touch the accelerator lightly when downshifting in order to rev the engine and make it easy to change gears.
Cf. drag down, grab one, kick down, lugging, overspeed, split the cogs.

feather hauler: **1**. a dry-freight hauler.
Cf. dry box, dry-freight.
2. a trucker who hauls light loads; often used by steel haulers in comparing themselves to other truckers, as steel haulers almost always haul the maximum legal weight.
Cf. balloon freight, iron hauler, load of postholes, painted scrap-iron hauler, zephyr haul.

feeder service: short truck runs from terminals into local areas to pick up and transport freight to a main collection point for a long run to another area or state.
Cf. bulk freight, claim, freight forwarder, interline, minnie.

fiddle: a radio in a tractor.
Syn.: hillbilly operahouse, noisemaker.

fifth over: a five-speed transmission that has an overdrive gear.
Cf. idiot transmission.

fifth wheel: the coupling device located on the tractor's rear frame that is used to join the front end of the trailer to the tractor. The fifth wheel is a flat, rounded plate with a V-shaped notch in the rear part. When the trucker hooks up to a trailer, the kingpin on the bottom of the trailer nose is locked into position at the apex of the V to allow it to be pulled without becoming uncoupled. The fifth wheel acts as a pivot point when the rig makes a turn; on the negative side, it contributes to the "jacknife potential" of winter driving.
Cf. air slider, break the unit, cup and saucer, inverted fifth wheel, jump the pin, sliding fifth wheel, unlatch.

fifty-mission cap: a trucker's hat that usually has several safety badges fastened to it.
Syn.: fifty-mission crush cap, gearshift cap.

fifty-mission crush hat: a trucker's cap that looks like the Air Force cap of the same name.
Syn.: fifty-mission cap, gearshift cap.
Cf. chain-drive wallet, double-clutchin' boots, split-shiftin' gloves.

fingerprint: to unload cargo by hand.
Syn.: hand job.
Cf. chimney sweep run, tailgate it.

fire it up: to start a diesel engine.
Syn.: build a fire, kick 'er over, shake down the ashes, wind 'er up.

fire wall: the partition between the tractor's engine and the driver's compartment in the cab.
Cf. dog box.

fishplate: a steel plate reinforcement on the outside of the truck frame to help it hold up under extra heavy hauling conditions.
Cf. gloving.

fishtail: a trailer will fishtail, or swing back and forth during travel, if the sliding tandems are too far forward and there is proportionately too much weight in the rear of the trailer.
Cf. sliding tandem, stretched out.

fishyback: the transportation by ship of an entire trailer intact with cargo.
Cf. birdyback, containerization, pig, piggyback.

five-and-two: a five-speed transmission with a two-speed rear axle.
Cf. fifth over, idiot transmission, three-speed axle, two-speed axle, unishift.

five-axle rig: a rig made up of a tandem-axle tractor and a tandem-axle trailer.
Syn.: eighteen-wheel rig, tandem-tandem.

Fix or Repair Daily: trucker's longhand for a Ford tractor, considered to be the bane of the driver's existence and the boon of the mechanic's.
Cf. **G**arage **M**an's **C**ompanion, In Hock Constantly, **R**uns **E**mpty **O**nly, two-story Falcon.

flagpoles: on a conventional cab, rods fastened to each end of the front bumper to help the driver judge his proximity to objects.

flagship: the best truck in a fleet.
Cf. dog catcher, rolling palace.

flame thrower: a rig that shows a flame at the end of its smokestack. Such a rig has too high a fuel-to-air ratio for proper running efficiency, and the wasted fuel ignites or smokes as it hits the air on exhaust.

Cf. build a fire, cut 'er down, lay a trail, set it up, throwin' flame, turn the wick up.

flat bed: a trailer with a platform for carrying freight but with no sides.

Syn.: flat bottom, flat deck, platform.

Cf. float, single-drop trailer.

flat bottom: a flat bed trailer usually used for hauling steel and metal products, which are chained to the bed and sometimes covered with a tarp lashed down to each side.

Syn.: flat deck, platform.

Cf. load her heavy on the high side, rub rails.

flat deck: a trailer with a freight-carrying platform but no sides or roof.

Cf. forty-foot flat, stretch flat.

flat face: a cabover tractor.

Syn.: blunt-nose, pug, snub-nose.

Cf. conventional cab.

flip top: a tilt-cab tractor.

Cf. alligator, tilt cab.

float: a flat bed trailer that has a unique device to make loading easy. Before the tractor is hooked up, the dollies retract, lowering the nose of the flat to the ground. The cargo is then loaded by sliding it up the lowered end. The flat is raised by means of a winch mounted on the rear of the tractor for this purpose.

Syn.: mud trailer.

Cf. winch rig.

floater: a driver without a steady job.

Cf. gypsy.

floating chrome: a decked-out tractor, one with many chromed accessories.

Syn.: all dolled up.

Cf. goodied up, hillbilly chrome, Kentucky chrome, rolling palace.

floats: large single tires used in place of duals.

Cf. peg leg, half axle.

float the gears: to shift gears without using the clutch.

Cf. clutch artist, split the cogs.

floorboard it: to accelerate by depressing the accelerator to its full extent, right down to the floorboards.

Syn.: big hole it, highball it, pour on the coals.

Cf. build a fire, tacked out, throttle shakes.

flyer: a run in which the driver takes a trailer to a distant terminal, leaves it, and pulls a second trailer back to the home terminal.

Cf. clock load, hot load, peddle run, pension run, red label load, turn around driver.

flying low: driving a truck at high speed.

Syn.: build a fire, burn the breeze, haul the mail, lean on it, run wide open.

flying orders: instructions given to a driver by his dispatcher.

Cf. brownie points, dedicated, delayed, dispatch.

follow the bulldog: to drive a Mack tractor, whose trademark and symbol is a bulldog.

Cf. anteater, B-model, cherry picker, Mack, sidewinder.

foot feed: the accelerator, as opposed to a hand throttle. Some tractors have both.
Cf. floorboard it, throttle shakes.

foot in the floorboards: to maintain a full-throttle operation.
Syn.: build a fire, floorboard it, big hole it, haul the mail, pour on the coals.

foot in the pump: to drive at a high r.p.m. in every gear or at a top overall speed. The word "pump" refers to the fuel pump of the engine.
Syn.: big hole it, build a fire, floorboard it, foot in the floorboards, haul the mail, pour on the coals.
Cf. top off, tacked out.

for-hire carrier: a carrier that transports property for a fee. Composed of local, intrastate and interstate truckers, the for-hire classification includes common carriers, contract carriers and exempt carriers. All must comply with I.C.C. safety, equipment and hours-of-service rules.
Cf. private carrier.

fork lift: a machine used to load and unload a truck. It has two long, heavy prongs that can raise and lower freight into position on the trailer.
Cf. dock monkey.

forty acres: humorously, the amount of space some truckers need in which to turn their rigs around.
Cf. need a hinge.

forty-foot flat: a flat bed trailer that is forty feet in length, a common variety of flat bed.
Cf. step-deck trailer.

forty grand: a payload weighing forty thousand pounds. "Grand" is used to mean thousand, and it is almost always used to refer to heavy loads in excess of forty thousand pounds. For instance, a trucker might speak of one load as weighing thirty-eight thousand but another as forty-three grand.
Cf. axle out a load, feather hauler, G.C.W., G.V.W., jag, over on the drive.

four-banger: a four-cylinder diesel engine.
Cf. banger, bucket, bumble bee, four-lunger, six-banger.

four-by-four: a transmission with four speeds in the main box and four in the auxiliary box.
Cf. four-way split, quad.

four-by-four: a single-axle tractor (Army use).
Cf. six-by-six, six-by-two.

four-laner: a trucker who prefers using multilane interstate highways to the exclusion, whenever possible, of smaller roads. The term is sometimes derogative.
Cf. back-pasture hauler, boondockin' cowpath, hot load, moonlighter.

four-lunger: a gas engine with four cylinders.
Cf. four-banger.

four thousand: the model CO-4000 International Harvester tractor, a cabover used extensively for over-the road work.
Cf. corn binder, Emeryville.

four-way relay emergency valve: the valve located below the trailer bed and in front of the tandems; composed of four hoses running into a valve, its purpose is to keep air from escaping from the trailer when a trucker disconnects the glad hands. Thus the four-way relay sets the trailer brakes, and not the tractor-protection valve, as is commonly believed.

Cf. tractor-protection valve.

four-way split: a four-speed auxiliary box in the transmission; so named because it has a four-way split in the gears.

Cf. quad, three-way split, two-way split.

four-wheeler: **1.** a short, four-wheel trailer.

Syn.: pup, kite.

Cf. kite without a tail.

2. a single-axle tractor, as opposed to a tandem-axle tractor.

Cf. eight-wheeler, six-wheeler, ten-wheeler.

free astray: a bill that covers an overflow of commodities scheduled for a certain destination when they are placed on a mixed truckload.

Cf. bill of lading, bulk freight, minnie.

free passes to bankruptcy: credit cards.

freight forwarder: a company that gathers small shipments into larger ones to form full trailer loads. Each full load is sent to a point where it is disassembled and the smaller loads sent on to their final destinations.

Cf. feeder service.

Freightliner: short for White Freightliner, one of the better makes of tractors.

Syn.: Fruitliner.

Cf. vanliner.

Frisco: San Francisco, California.

Cf. Big Town, Dago.

frogging: increasing engine speed and suddenly engaging the clutch; not a good practice for a driver to follow because he could break an axle or twist a drive shaft.

front PTO: an adapting device on the front of the crankshaft usually used on cement mixers to supply auxiliary power (**p**ower **t**ake**o**ff) to the rotational body of the mixer.

Cf. split-shaft PTO.

front wheel eliminating valve: a valve that can be set to eliminate fifty percent of the air that operates the front wheel brakes; used when traveling in slippery weather because full brake application on wet roads can cause skidding. When the valve is set at "dry road," the front wheels have full braking power; when it is set at "slippery road," the braking power is reduced.

Cf. air brakes, air pressure gauge, slack adjuster.

frost law: a law that lowers axle weight and gross combination weight allowances when the frost starts coming out of the ground in the spring.

Cf. mud season.

Fruitliner: truckese for a White Freightliner tractor.

Cf. Awful-car, Detroit vibrator, KantWork, Mexican Freightliner, rinky dink.

fuel gauge: the gauge on the tractor's instrument panel that indicates the amount of fuel in the tanks. A diesel rig draws fuel from both tanks at once: when the gauge reads half full, each tank is half full. A gas rig draws from one tank at a time and normally empties the left tank first to eliminate danger in a sideswipe accident.

Cf. full saddles, saddle tanks.

fuel stop: a service station where truckers stop to fuel up their rigs, as opposed to a truck stop where a restaurant, sleeping accommodations and many other services are available to truckers.

Cf. coffee pot, truck-o-tel, truck stop.

full cap: a tire recap of both the road-surface area and the sides of the tire.

Cf. cap.

full-floating axle: an axle that is suspended in its housing and in which the load and wheel stress is supported by the housing rather than by the axle.

Cf. axle, semi-floating axle.

full mount: the practice of placing an entire car, pickup truck, tractor or trailer on a semi-trailer, usually a flat or lowboy, to transport it to another area.

Cf. double deck, double mount, saddle mount, triple deck, triple mount.

full saddles: rectangular fuel tanks that wrap over a tractor's frame to the rear of the cab. The part that runs over the frame also holds fuel.

Cf. saddle tanks, step tanks.

full screw: a tandem-drive tractor, one in which both rear axles actively pull, as opposed to a power unit with only one live axle.

Syn.: both axles pulling, two axles pulling, tandem drive, twin screw.

Cf. dead axle, drivers, pushers, spider.

full-throttle operation: to run a rig at top speed.

full trailer: a trailer with both front and rear axles; used as the second trailer in a double-bottom rig or hooked behind a straight truck to form a truck-trailer combination. A semi-trailer can be converted into a full trailer by the addition of dollies (converting gear).

Cf. converter dolly, semi and pup, train, truck-trailer.

furniture van body: a trailer specifically designed for the transportation of household goods. Such a van usually has a floor that is lower, between the axles of the tractor and the axles of the trailer, than it is directly over the axles in order to increase the cubic capacity of the van.

Cf. bedbug hauler, bull nose, mountain climbin' job.

F.W.D.: a company that manufactures **f**ront-**w**heel **d**rive tractors, snow plows, dump trucks, and other such vehicles. In addition, F.W.D. is the original manufacturer of front-wheel drive vehicles.

Cf. six-by-six.

G

gallop: when a tractor "gallops," every wheel tends to jump up and down because the brake drums and wheels are not balanced. It often occurred in older rigs; these days, truck wheels, drive shafts and brake drums are better balanced.

galloping: a fluctuation in an engine's revolutions per minute while the engine idles.
Syn.: hunting, loping.

galloping irons: connecting rods in a motor.
Cf. ventilate the motor.

gandy dancer: a weaving truck.
Cf. dog track, lane hopper.

Garage Man's Companion: humorous nickname for a tractor manufactured by General Motors Corporation.
Syn.: **G**eneral **M**ess of **C**rap, **G**ood **M**ountain **C**limber, Hillbilly Special, Jamie, Jimmy.
Cf. Detroit Diesel, screamin' Lena.

garbage hauler: a trucker who hauls vegetables or fruit. Usually not used by a trucker in referring to himself.
Syn.: produce hauler.
Cf. bean hauler, green stuff.

gas job: a tractor that runs on gasoline instead of diesel fuel.
Cf. bubble burner, juice jockey, oil burner, smoker.

gateway: **1.** the beginning of a turnpike at a state line.
2. a point where freight is exchanged between different truck lines.
Cf. connecting carrier.
3. a point through which a trucker must pass to comply with his company's operating authorities.

G.C.W.: the **G**ross **C**ombination **W**eight of a tractor-trailer and its cargo. Each state has a different method for determining how much weight each truck may carry, but a common method is to allot so much weight per axle (thus it follows that a five-axle rig can carry much more weight than a three-axle rig). This situation is annoying to a long-distance trucker because in one state his G.C.W. may be legal, but not his rig's overall length; in the next, he may be a few tons overweight, and in the neighboring state he may be running legally in all respects.

Cf. axle out a load, axle weight, curb weight, forty grand, G.V.W., over on the drive.

gear bonger: a trucker who heedlessly grinds gears while shifting.

Syn.: cog stripper, gear jammer.

Cf. clutch artist, scratch one in, sheep herder.

gearboxes: some trucks have two gearboxes: a main box, which controls the speed (as in second gear), and an auxiliary box which controls the level of that speed (in second gear, second low or second high). Such trucks have four or five speeds in the main box and from two to four in the auxiliary; total forward speeds range from eight to twenty, and from two to four in reverse, depending on the transmission.

Cf. aux box, brownie, deep-reduction valve, duplex, main box, mix-master special, overdrive, quadriplex, skip gears, Spicer, splitter, three-speed axle, triplex, two-speed axle, unishift.

gear jammer: **1.** a driver who usually clashes gears.
Syn.: cog stripper, gear bonger.
Cf. boll weevil, clutch artist, sheep herder.
2. generally speaking, any truck driver.
Syn.: big rig man, distribution technician, gear shifter, spinner.

gearship cap: a trucker's hat.
Syn.: fifty-mission cap, fifty-mission crush hat.
Cf. double-clutchin' boots, split-shiftin' gloves.

gear shifter: a trucker.
Syn.: big rig man, double-clutchin' man, gear jammer, line driver, semi driver.

General Mess of Crap: humorous nickname for a tractor manufactured by General Motors Corporation.
Syn.: **G**arage **M**an's **C**ompanion, **G**ood **M**ountain **C**limber, Jamie, Jimmy, Hillbilly Special.
Cf. Detroit Diesel, screamin' Lena.

Georgia overdrive: the neutral gear position; used when a driver, going downhill, throws the tractor out of gear and allows it to coast.
Syn.: eleventh gear, Jewish overdrive, Mexican overdrive, midnight overdrive, thirteenth gear.
Cf. whistlin' gear.

gesundheit starter: an air-powered starter; named for the "sneezing" noise a tractor makes when its air starter is activated.
Cf. blow him up, kick 'er over, wind 'er up.

gettin' it done: making time or going down the road in style.
Syn: big hole it, build a fire, floorboard it, haul

the mail, highball it, pour on the coals, tacked out.

gettin' stretched: working a tractor up to and running it at its top speed.

Syn.: all stretched out, big hole it, build a fire, tacked out, top off, turn it on.

Cf. back off.

get with it: to do anything the way it should be done; for instance, shifting gears.

Cf. scratch one in.

gin poles: two poles on a winch rig that, when raised into position, form an A-frame that is used for winching and lifting.

Cf. winch rig.

gippo: **1.** a trucker who will haul any load anywhere for anyone.

Syn.: gypsy, moonlighter, wildcatter.

2. derogatorily, another trucker, especially if his rig is in poor shape.

give her the works: **1.** to crank a starter on an old-fashioned truck.

Syn.: shake down the ashes.

Cf. armstrong starter, stew winder.

2. to start up a truck.

Syn.: build a fire, kick 'er over, wind 'er up.

give him the lights: to help a driver who is passing on the road by flicking the headlights to inform him when he has ample clearance to pull back into the right lane. The passing driver should acknowledge the courtesy by flashing his own clearance lights in return. Light signals are used in a variety of circumstances. A driver may flash his lights at an oncoming rig to warn the driver to slow down because of a radar unit or an accident on the road ahead. He may also signal another driver that the other's headlights, fog lights or running lights are not functioning.

Cf. give him the windup, shake the lights, smoke him.

give him the wind: to signal an oncoming trucker that the road ahead is clear and that he can safely speed up without fear of running into radar units or heavy traffic. Different hand signals are used to inform other drivers of a radar unit on the road ahead, an open weighing station (the nightmare of truckers with overweight rigs), a logbook check by officials, a lady hitchhiker, and so on.

Syn.: give him the windup

Cf. give him the lights.

give him the windup: to signal an oncoming trucker that the road ahead is clear and that he can safely speed up his rig without fear of encountering heavy traffic or a radar unit.

Syn.: give him the wind.

Cf. give him the lights, shake the lights.

give it a douche job: **1.** to wash a truck.

2. to steam-clean a trailer—a legal necessity when hauling fish or unprocessed meat.

Cf. douche bag.

glad hand: an air-line connection between the tractor and the trailer.

Syn.: handshake.

Cf. air hose, pigtail, pogo stick, trolley lines.

gloving: metal reinforcement of a truck's chassis

if the reinforcement is made on both sides of the frame.

Cf. fishplate.

goat: usually a homemade straight job; a small truck, used to gather fruit, that has a hoist to lift the body to the height of the fruit and to tilt the body for discharging the fruit.

Cf. tipper.

goathorns: twin exhaust stacks that are curved at the top so that the exhaust exits to the side instead of straight up into the air.

Syn.: buckhorn pipes.

Cf. bark, gutted, smitty, smokestack, spittoon muffler, twin chimneys, woodpecker.

go-away gear: the highest gear or the highest combination of gears in the gearbox.

Syn.: goin' home gear, pay hole, whistlin' gear.

Cf. grandma gear.

goin' down: a truck going from the northern part of the United States toward the South is said to be "goin' down."

Cf. goin' up.

goin' home gear: the highest combination of gears in a transmission, probably christened in honor of the zealous haste truckers make when headed home.

Syn.: go-away gear, goin' home hole, pay hole.

goin' home hole: the highest gear or combination of gears in a truck's transmission.

Syn.: big hole, go-away gear, goin' home gear, pay hole, whistlin' gear.

goin' up: said of a truck headed north out of the South.

Cf. goin' down.

goodied up: a tractor with many driver luxuries, such as an air conditioner, stereo and a television in the bunk.

Syn.: rolling palace.

Cf. decked out, floating chrome, zebra stripes.

Good Mountain Climber: a tractor manufactured by the General Motors Corporation, somewhat sarcastically nicknamed because a GMC tractor often likes to takes its time when it comes to a hill or mountain.

Syn.: **G**arage **M**an's **C**ompanion, **G**reat **M**ountain **C**limber, **G**eneral **M**ess of **C**rap, Jamie, Jimmy.

goo-guard: fenders or splash shields installed on a tractor in front of the wheels to prevent mud and small stones from hitting and damaging the tractor.

Cf. shroud.

goose it: to choke the engine, to feed it a richer fuel-to-air mixture.

Cf. gun the motor, hand throttle, turn the wick up.

gooseneck: the curved section of a trailer frame that includes the kingpin and the fifth wheel apron.

Cf. detachable gooseneck, drop frame, lowboy, pot belly.

gooseneck lowboy: a lowboy trailer that has an extended "neck" that couples over the fifth wheel of the tractor. Most commonly used for the transportation of construction machinery or farm equipment.

Cf. detachable gooseneck, double-drop trailer, level deck lowboy, outriggers.

governor: a device installed in the carburetor or fuel pump to limit the engine's revolutions per minute and hence the vehicle's speed.

Cf. cut 'er down, set it up.

grab a gear: to downgear a transmission in an effort to gain power.

Syn.: grab one.

Cf. drop gears, drag down, knock it down.

grab a handful of air: to apply the brakes.

Syn.:clamp on the binders, grab some air, reach for the air, spike it, throw out the anchor.

Cf. dynamite the brakes.

grab handle: **1.** the handle on the front of a tractor that enables a garageman to clean the windshield. **2.** a handle on the side of the tractor to assist the driver in entering.

grab one: to shift into a lower gear to gain power when ascending a hill.

Syn.: grab a gear.

Cf. drop gears, drag down, feather, kick down, knock it down.

grab some air: to apply the brakes.

Syn.: grab a handful of air, reach for the air, throw out the anchor.

Cf. trolley-valve handle.

grab some gears: to drive a truck.

Cf. eatin' concrete, make some miles, wheel a rig.

grain body: a low-sided trailer with an open top

that is used to transport dry fluid commodities such as grain.

Cf. hopper body.

grandfather rights: the original certification of hauling rights issued by the I.C.C. in 1935. Covering the types of commodities hauled and the rights to haul into specific areas, the certification served to "freeze" the rights then currently held; they were originally designed to restrict the number of haulers without depriving them of their existing rights.

Cf. tariff.

grandma gear: the lowest combination of gears in a transmission.

Syn.: creeper gear, down in the kitchen, growler, ought hole.

Cf. big hole, pulling gear, wobbly hole.

granny rag: **1.** a red one-foot-square overwide flag used to demarcate an overdimensional load.

Cf. overdimensional load, permit. **2.** a rag used to check oil or to wipe off a driver's hands.

Cf. church key.

gravy hauler: a driver who hauls high-paying loads.

Cf. brownie points, milk run, pension run.

gray operator: 1. a truck line that operates just within the law.

Cf. broker, gypsy, moonlighter, owner-operator, wildcat.

2. an independent trucker, one who personally contracts for the freight he hauls.

Syn.: gypsy, wildcatter.

grease monkey: a mechanic in a truck stop who greases or works on trucks.
Cf. chief hood lifter, ice man, maniac.

greasy spoon: a run-down truck stop.
Syn.: choke and puke, pigpen, heartburn palace.
Cf. pig.

Great Mountain Climber: any tractor made by the General Motors Corporation.
Syn.: **G**arage **M**an's **C**ompanion, **G**eneral **M**ess of **C**rap, Hillbilly Special, Jimmy.
Cf. Awful-car, Dirge, Fruitliner, **F**ix **o**r **R**epair **D**aily, KantWork, **R**uns **E**mpty **O**nly.

green stuff: green perishables or produce, such as lettuce, cucumbers and radishes.
Cf. garbage hauler, produce hauler.

gross weight: the weight of a truck or of a tractor-trailer together with the weight of its entire contents.
Cf. curb weight, G.C.W., G.V.W.

grounded: **1.** a driver is grounded when his license is revoked.
Cf. cowboy, Sears-Roebuck license.
2. a truck may be grounded if it fails to pass the mandatory I.C.C. safety inspection.
Cf. out of service.

growler: the lowest combination of gears in a transmission.
Syn.: creeper gear, grandma gear, number-one hole.
Cf. big hole, pay hole, wobbly hole.

grunt-and-squeal jockey: a trucker who hauls bulls or hogs.

Syn.: shoat and goat conductor.

Cf. bull rack, cackle crate, Pork Chop Express.

gumball machine: the warning light on the roof of a highway patrol car or any emergency car.

Syn.: bubble gum machine.

Cf. believer, big hat, bird dog, vulture.

gumballs: ether packaged in ball form to be used to start a diesel engine in cold weather.

Syn.: mothballs.

Cf. ether lock.

gun it: to race the motor.

Syn.: gun the motor.

Cf. can the motor, goose it.

gunny sack job: a badly used, dilapidated truck.

Syn.: bucket of bolts, clunker, crate, dog, iron, junker, residenter.

Cf. been around the Horn.

gun the motor: to race the engine.

Syn.: gun it.

gutless wonder: a truck that will not pull a load.

Syn.: dog, drag, sick horse.

Cf. dog catcher, husky oat motor, oakie blower, supercharger, turbocharger.

gutted: said of an exhaust stack when the trucker has removed the interior baffles placed there to reduce the amount of noise the engine makes.

Cf. bark, build a fire, goathorns, smitty, smokestack, spittoon muffler, twin chimneys.

G.V.W.: **G**ross **V**ehicle **W**eight, the weight of an empty tractor or trailer.

Cf. curb weight, G.C.W.

gypsy: an independent trucker, one who leases his outfit to any one he can get a load from.

Syn.: gippo, moonlighter, wildcatter.
Cf. boondockin', floater, runnin' hot.

H

half axle: the first rear axle on a tandem-axle tractor when it has only single tires and not duals.
Syn.: peg leg.
Cf. floats, pusher, spider.

half cab: originally, the over-the-road tractor manufactured by Kenworth in 1956. The driver's compartment extended only part of the way over the right side of the tractor, as opposed to a full-size cabover, the compartment of which extends the full width of the tractor. This model was designed to cut down on the vehicle's weight and to make access to the engine easy; it was used to haul cranes or any excessively long cargo, which rested alongside of the driver's compartment.
Cf. alligator, flip top.
Cf. straight.

hand job: a cargo that must be unloaded by hand by the trucker or by a dock walloper.
Cf. chimney sweep run, fingerprint, tailgate it.

handshake: the metal clasp on the side of the air line connections between the tractor and the trailer. The trailer has a complementary handshake permanently mounted on it that acts as a counterpart to that on the tractor; when the air lines are hooked up, they look as if they are shaking hands.
Syn.: glad hand.

Cf. air hose, pogo stick, trolley lines.

hand throttle: a manually set throttle in a tractor that is used to maintain a certain engine speed.
Cf. foot feed, turn the wick up.

hand valve: the valve that controls only the trailer brakes.
Syn.: monkey bar, trolley-valve handle.
Cf. Johnson bar, West Coast hookup.

hanging up: said of the brakes of either the tractor or the trailer when they fail to release.
Cf. California air, low-air warning device, tractor-protection valve, slack adjuster.

hard pedal: to use a hard braking action,
Cf. dynamite the brakes, front wheel eliminating valve, jacknife, set 'er down, soft pedal.

hauling postholes: running without cargo.
Syn.: deadhead.
Cf. back haul, load of postholes.

haul the mail: to speed up or make up for lost time.
Syn.: big hole it, build a fire, floorboard it, gettin' it done, highball it, pour it on.
Cf. smoke him, tacked out.

headache rack: the heavy meshwork grill on the rear of a cab that protects it from damage from a load that may shift forward in the event of a suddent stop or accident.
Cf. bulkhead.

header bar: a hinged rear crosspiece on an open top trailer that can be swung to one side to allow the loading of high cargo, then locked back into position to form part of the frame for the trailer doors.

header board: the shield at the front of a flat bed trailer that prevents the load from shifting forward and striking the rear of the cab.
Syn.: bulkhead.
Cf. headache rack.

heartburn palace: a truck stop or diner noted for its second-rate food.
Syn.: choke and puke, greasy spoon, pigpen.
Cf. coffee pot, fuel stop, truck stop.

heavy hauler: a carrier of unusually heavy or over-size commodities that require special equipment for loading, shipping and unloading.
Cf. carrier, specialized carrier.

helpers: stay-awake pills; extralegal stimulants used by some truckers to maintain peak alertness on an extra long or rigorous haul.
Syn.: copilots.
Cf. bennie, eye trouble, L.A. turnaround, Upjohns.

herd: to drive a truck.
Syn.: grab some gears, make some miles, push a rig, truck, wheel a rig.
Cf. eatin' concrete.

highballer: a driver who customarily drives at or near top speed.
Syn.: aviator, lead foot.
Cf. barrel on down the road, foot in the floorboards, pour on the coals, smokin' in high gear.

highball it: to drive a tractor-trailer at or near its top speed.
Syn.: big hole it, floorboard it, pour it on.
Cf. aviator, highballer, lead foot.

high cube: refers to a trailer with exceptional cubic foot capacity, usually with dropped frames and thin walls, and usually used for moving furniture and household goods.
Cf. cube, drop bottom.

high side: the higher speed in a two-speed auxiliary transmission.
Cf. direct, duplex, low side, two-way split.

high split: the highest speed in a three-speed aux box.
Cf. brownie, high side, low split, over and under overdrive, three-way split, triplex.

hillbilly chrome: aluminum paint, rather than chrome, on a tractor's wheels or smokestacks.
Cf. floating chrome, truck-stop commando.

hillbilly operahouse: a tractor with a radio; so named because many drivers listen to hillbilly music stations.
Syn.: fiddle, noisemaker.

Hillbilly Special: a General Motors Corporation tractor.
Syn.: **G**eneral **M**ess of **C**rap, Jamie, Jimmy, poor man's tractor.
Cf. Detroit Diesel, match box Jimmy, screamin' Lena.

hitchhiker: a projection on the rear of a tractor that keeps the air lines and electric cable from dragging between the tractor and the trailer.
Syn.: pogo stick.
Cf. glad hand, headache rack, pigtail, trailer connections.

hobo: a tractor that is shifted from one terminal to another.
Cf. switcher.

hog hauler: a trucker who transports swine; used in a derogatory sense, any livestock hauler.
Syn.: grunt-and-squeal jockey, shoat and goat conductor.
Cf. bull hauler, cackle crate, meat hauler, Pork Chop Express, possum belly, shoat boat, weeder geese hauler.

hole: a shift position in a gear box.
Cf. big hole, go-away gear, number-one hole, mixing stick, wobbly hole.

holy road: a broken-up highway with many potholes.
Syn.: religious road.
Cf. berm, line, spooks.

honey bucket: a truck equipped with a tank used to clean septic tanks.
Syn.: honey wagon.
Cf. honey dipper.

honey dipper: an operator who cleans septic tanks or cesspools.
Cf. honey wagon.

honey wagon: a truck with a tank used to clean out septic tanks.
Syn.: honey bucket.

hood lifter: a garage mechanic.
Syn.: maniac.
Cf. chief hood lifter, grease monkey, ice man, sledgehammer mechanic.

hoo-hooer: a driver who uses the air horn to excess.
Cf. trumpet.

hook 'er into high: to shift into high gear.
Cf. goin' home hole, payhole, split the cogs, tacked out, top off, whistlin' gear.

hook up: to couple a tractor to a trailer.

Cf. break the unit, drop it on the nose, jump the pin, unlatch.

hopper body: a sectionalized trailer body capable of being unloaded through a bottom opening; not tilted to ease unloading, as a dump body is.
Cf. bottom dumps, side dump.

horse: the tractor, or power unit, of a tractor-trailer combination.
Cf. loose horse, mill, power plant, sick horse.

horse light: a spotlight mounted on the cab to reveal open range livestock (Texas usage).
Syn.: cattle light, house number hunters, name plate finders.
Cf. coon light, twin spots.

horses: engine horsepower.
Cf. husky oat motor, mill, oakie blower, power plant, turbocharger.

hot foot: a brake shoe, made of a steel-magnesium alloy, that is popular in the West.
Syn.: hot shoe, mag brake, steely.
Cf. Emma Jesse brake, jack-off bar, sucker brake.

hot load: **1.** a rush shipment of cargo.
Cf. clock load, flyer, swinger.
2. a cargo of illegitimate merchandise.
Cf. back-pasture hauler, boondockin', moonlighter, Moonlight Express, runnin' hot.

hot mix: hot asphalt in transit to a building site.
Cf. front PTO, split-shaft PTO.

hot shoe: a brake shoe, made of a steel-magnesium alloy, that is popular in hilly areas because the hotter a hot shoe becomes, the better it brakes the truck.

Syn.: hot foot, mag brake, steely.
Cf. Jake brake.

Hound: a Greyhound bus.
Cf. dog catcher.

hour meter: an instrument that indicates the total number of hours a truck engine has been run.
Cf. milograph, tachograph, tachometer, odometer.

household goods mover: a trucker who drives for a furniture-moving company.
Syn.: bedbug hauler, relocation consultant.
Cf. mountain climbin' job.

house number hunters: cab-mounted spotlights used by truckers to find an address on a building at night.
Cf. nameplate finders.

hub-o-meter: an odometer that is mounted outside of the rear drive wheel and the variety used by most leasing companies.
Cf. milograph, squealer.

hump-back trailer: a trailer body whose floor curves upward in the middle; an aluminum flat bed trailer, for example, curves upward when it is empty.

hundred-mile coffee: coffee strong enough to keep a driver alert for at least one hundred miles; the universal beverage of gear jammers.
Cf. bedsteader, coffee pot, copilots, bennie chaser, eye trouble.

hungry boards: side boards used on a dump trailer to raise the sides and thereby increase the carrying capacity; so named because a trucker using them must be "hungry" for money.

Syn.: cheater boards, side boards.

Cf. bathtub dump, struck capacity, water-level hauling capacity.

Hunter heater: a heater that operates on a separate gas tank and is used to warm the truck's interior.

Cf. eskimo.

hunting: a fluctuation or variation in an engine's revolutions per minute while it is idling.

Syn.: galloping, loping.

husky oat motor: a high-horsepower engine.

Cf. dog catcher, gutless wonder, oakie blower, power plant, supercharger, turbocharger.

hydraulic brakes: a braking system that depends on the transmission of hydraulic pressure from a master cylinder to the wheel cylinders.

Cf. air brakes, air-over-hydraulic brakes, push 'n' wonder brakes, sucker brake.

I

I.B.T.: short for the International Brotherhood of Teamsters, Chauffeurs, Warehousemen & Helpers of America, better known as the Teamsters Union.

Cf. Teamster.

I-Can-Catch: humorous nickname for the **I**nterstate **C**ommerce **C**ommission.

Cf. I-men, **D**eath **O**n **T**ruckers.

ice box: **1.** a refrigerated trailer used for hauling produce and perishables.

Syn.: cold box, ice wagon, reefer.

Cf. dry box.

2. the bunker for ice in a bunk-and-blower type cooling system in an insulated trailer.

Cf. cold blow, ice man, putt-putt.

ice man: a Thermo King mechanic or any refrigeration man who works on reefer trailers.

Cf. ice box, hood lifter, grease monkey, maniac.

ice wagon: a refrigerated trailer.

Syn.: cold box, ice box, reefer.

Cf. bunker, ice man, putt-putt.

identification lights: the cluster of three clearance lights at the top center of the tractor and on the rear top of the trailer.

Cf. bus markers, Christmas tree, horse light, rolling lighthouse, running lights, torpedoes.

idiot light: a small light sometimes found on the front end of a tractor, the light turns on when the ignition is started.

Cf. Christmas tree, identification lights.

idiot lights: the lights on a truck's dash which may inform the driver that: 1) the turn signal is on, 2) there is low oil pressure, 3) the emergency brake is on, 4) there is low air pressure, 5) the generator is not charging, (6) the high beams are on.

idiot transmission: the five-and-two transmission with an overdrive gear; so named because in shifting this transmission, the order is first low, first high, second low, second high, third low, third high, fourth low, fifth low, fourth high, fifth high. The name comes from the truckers' saying that "Only an idiot would put fifth low in front of fourth high."

Cf. fifth over, two-speed axle.

I-men: investigators from the Interstate Commerce Commission.

Cf. believer, big hat, Death On Truckers, gumball machine.

Indian talk: diesel smoke coming from a smokestack or exhaust pipe.

Cf. lay a trail, smoker, throwin' flame.

In Hock Constantly: humorous expression for the financial condition of any owner-operator who has a tractor manufactured by **I**nternational **H**arvester **C**ompany.

Cf. Bifocal International, corn binder, Emeryville, **F**ix **O**r **R**epair **D**aily, **G**arage **M**an's **C**ompanion, **R**uns **E**mpty **O**nly, West Coast binder.

initial carrier: the trucking line that picks up a shipment from a shipper.

Cf. connecting carrier, freight forwarder, interline.

injector: the mechanism that injects fuel into the cylinder of a diesel engine.

Cf. banger, diesel, percolator.

insulated body: a trailer designed to transport cargo that must be kept at a specific temperature. Such a trailer may be equipped for either heating or refrigeration.

Cf. green stuff, reefer.

intercity driver: a driver who drives within city limits only.

Syn.: local driver.

Cf. over-the-road driver, semi driver.

interline: to move freight from its point of origin to its destination by using the authorities of two or more trucking lines.

Cf. connecting carrier, gateway, initial carrier, trip lease.

Interstate Commerce Commission: the federal rule-making body which regulates the rates, charges and practices of interstate carriers and enforces federal laws and regulations governing employees, mode of operation, rates and routes of common, contract and exempt carriers. It also regulates the hauling of explosives and other dangerous cargoes and investigates drivers' hours, activities while on the road and fitness to drive.

Cf. bible, copilots, grandfather rights, I-Can-Catch, I-men, log book, Moonlight Express, P.U.C., tariff, V.C.R.

intrastate shipping: any transportation of goods that has its origin and destination within the same state and that at no time crosses a state line.

Cf. P.U.C.

inverted fifth wheel: a fifth wheel attached to the trailer instead of to the tractor.

Cf. air slider, cup and saucer, removable king-pin.

iron: any old truck.

Syn.: been around the Horn, bucket of bolts, crate, gunny sack, job, junker.

iron hauler: a steel hauler.

Syn.: steel jockey.

Cf. painted scrap-iron hauler, feather hauler, Pig Iron Express, suicide coil..

iron lunger: the old model HRB Cummins engine.

Cf. diesel, gas job.

irons: snow tires or chains.
Cf. baloneys, put on the iron, rags, sanders, waffles.

J

jacking it around: backing a semi-trailer around a sharp curve.
Cf. boss her, dock it, need a hinge.

jackknife: to place the trailer at a sharp angle to the tractor. If a truck jackknifes in an accident (usually because of a sudden swerve or fast stop on a wet or icy road), the trailer skids around and hits the tractor.
Cf. belly up, pile up, total it out, widow-maker.

jack-off bar: the emergency brake handle.
Syn.: emerjensen, Emma Jesse brake, Johnson bar.
Cf. air brakes, California air, hand valve, hot shoe, Jake brake, sucker brake.

jag: a small cargo or pay load.
Cf. forty grand, load of postholes, L.T.L., minnie, part load, zephyr haul.

Jake brake: the Jacobs engine brake, which may be used as an auxiliary slowing device on a tractor. Named for inventor John Jacobson, the brake worked by closing off the exhaust pipe. This built up back pressure by preventing the exhaust from escaping and made the engine unwind more slowly. Used mostly on West Coast rigs because of the more mountainous terrain in the west.
Cf. California air, mag brake, West Coast hookup.

Jamie: any tractor manufactured by General Motors Corporation.
Syn.: **G**arage **M**an's **C**ompanion, Hillbilly Special, Jimmy, poor man's tractor, screamin' Lena.

Japanese Freightliner: the model 5000 White tractor. Nicknamed as a takeoff on the White Freightliner, it is to be carefully differentiated from the latter.
Syn.: Mexican Freightliner.
Cf. Fruitliner.

Jewish overdrive: the neutral gear position; used when a trucker, in driving downhill, throws the transmission out of gear and allows the rig to coast down.
Syn.: eleventh gear, Georgia overdrive, Mexican overdrive, midnight overdrive, thirteenth gear.

Jifflox dolly: a coupling device composed of an axle, wheels and a fifth wheel that can convert a single-axle tractor to a tandem; most noted for its use with International Harvester's Unistar four-wheel-drive tractor in pulling double-bottom combinations. The tractor is used as a single axle and the Jifflox dolly is used under the second trailer when doubles are desired; the dolly can be hooked to the tractor when the driver wants to pull a single trailer.
Syn.: converter dolly, double hookup, joe dog, jo-jo, whippletree.
Cf. double-bottom rig, kite without a tail, semi and pup, twin trailers.

Jimmy: a tractor manufactured by the General

Motors Corporation; the nickname comes from pronouncing the initials "GMC."
Syn.: **G**arage **M**an's **C**ompanion, **G**eneral **M**ess of **C**rap, **G**ood **M**ountain **C**limber, Hillbilly Special, Jamie, poor man's tractor, screamin' Jimmy, screamin' Lena.
Cf. Detroit Diesel.

joe dog: a device with a dead axle that converts a single-axle tractor into a tandem-axle tractor. It hooks over the tractor's fifth wheel, replacing it with another for the semi to be hooked onto.
Syn.: Jifflox dolly.

Johnson bar: the emergency brake handle; named after the old-time brakes on the pioneer trucks of the 1930s and 1940s, which were applied manually with a four-foot-long lever. Today the Johnson bar is a much shorter handle that is connected by cable to the brakes.
Syn.: emerjensen, jack-off bar.
Cf. air brakes.

jo-jo: a set of wheels equipped with a fifth wheel that is attached to the rear of a semi in order to couple another semi on behind.
Syn.: converter dolly, double hookup, whippletree.
Cf. joe dog.

jughandle: a type of intersection found in New Jersey formed by a lane from the right-hand side of the road that curves away from the highway and then crosses it at right angles. A jughandle, named for its appearance, enables traffic to make a left-hand turn or a U-

turn without blocking the left-hand lane of traffic on the highway.
Syn.: dog leg.
Cf. berm, holy road, line, spooks.

juice jockey: a trucker whose tractor runs on gasoline fuel generally a small tractor of comparatively lower power than a diesel rig.
Cf. bubble burner, diesel, gas job, oil burner, smoker.

juicepot: the carburetor in a gas engine.
Syn.: percolator.
Cf. injector.

jump seats: to change tractors with every run; said of the driver.
Cf. relay, slip-seat operation, switch seats.

jump the pin: to miss the trailer's kingpin when hooking a tractor to a trailer.
Cf. break the unit, drop the box, fifth wheel, kingpin, pull the pin.

junker: a shabby, worn truck.
Syn.: bucket of bolts, crate, dog, gunny sack job, residenter.
Cf. road bum, strip her.

K

KantWork: humorous nickname for a Kenworth tractor.
Syn.: katydid, kay wobbler, Kennie, KW.
Cf. Texas KW.

katydid: a Kenworth tractor.
Syn.: Kant Work, kay wobbler, Kennie, KW.
Cf. half cab, Kant Work, Texas KW.

kay wobbler: a Kenworth tractor.
Syn.: Kant Work katydid, Kennie, KW.
Cf. rolling palace.

keep 'er winding: to keep a truck's engine wound up tight against the governor; not to lug an engine.
Cf. drag down, grab one, lugging, overspeed, tachometer, windmill.

Kennie: nickname for a Kenworth tractor, the alleged Rolls-Royce of the trucking world, and comparable in its luxurious quality.
Syn.: katydid, kay wobbler.

Kentucky chrome: aluminum-painted trim on a tractor, usually on the wheels or smokestacks, as opposed to real chrome.
Syn.: hillbilly chrome.
Cf. floating chrome, truck stop commando.

kick down: to shift to a lower gear.
Syn.: drop gears, grab one, knock it down.
Cf. drag down, kick 'em, split the cogs.

kick 'em: to shift gears.
Syn.: split the cogs.
Cf. double-clutching, split-shifting.

kick 'er over: to start the engine.
Syn.: build a fire, fire it up, shake down the ashes, wind 'er up.
Cf. armstrong starter, crank, gesundheit starter, stew winder, turn the wick up.

kick the doughnuts: to check the tires of a truck.
Cf. baloneys, cheater slicks, irons, pumpkin, rider, tire billy.

kidney buster: a hard-riding truck, generally a cabover, because the driver's compartment, being over the steering axle, receives more of the jolt and vibration than it does in a conventional cab.

Syn: bone crusher.

Cf. air ride.

kingpin: the bolt on the underside of the front of a trailer that fits into the tractor's fifth wheel to couple the tractor and the trailer together.

Cf. jump the pin, pin setting, pull the pin, unlatch, removable kingpin.

kit: the frame, front end, cab and electrical connections used to rebuild an older model tractor or one that has been wrecked. The engine and rear end are salvaged from the older tractor and incorporated into the new one. Kits are usually Peterbilt, Kenworth or White Freightliner cabs.

kite: a four-wheeled trailer that has a short wheelbase.

Syn.: four-wheeler, pup.

Cf. kite without a tail, semi and pup.

kite without a tail: as opposed to a semi and pup, this is a semi-trailer with a set of dollies attached to the rear but without the pup trailer; usually seen when the trucker has dropped the pup or a second semi in a double-bottom rig and is driving to another destination.

Cf. jo-jo, kite, semi and pup, short bottom, train, whippletree.

knocked down: said of machinery or freight that is shipped in an unassembled state.

Cf. bulk freight.

knock it down: to downgear.

Syn.: drop gears, grab one, kick down.

Cf. drag down, split the cogs, tack.

KW: short for Kenworth, a make of tractor.
Syn.: katydid, kay wobbler, Kennie.
Cf. half cab, Texas KW.

L

L.A.: Los Angeles, California.
Cf. Bean Town, Big Town, Chi, Dago, Frisco.

lading: the freight in a truck.
Cf. bill of lading, bulk freight, minnie, tariff.

landing gear: the retractable supports on a trailer that prop up the front end when the trailer is unhitched from the tractor.
Syn.: dollies.
Cf. drop it on the nose, fifth wheel, kingpin, pull the pin.

lane hopper: a trucker who ignores traffic lines.
Cf. cowboy, real amateur, truck jockey, road hog.

L.A. turnaround: one of the strongest of the stay-awake pills; a user can allegedly turn Los Angeles without going to sleep once.
Syn.: West Coast turnaround.
Cf. bennie, copilots, eye trouble, helpers, Upjohns.

lay a trail: to emit a great amount of diesel smoke; said of a tractor.
Cf. Indian talk, smoker, throwin' flame.

lay her over: to turn the steering wheel slightly toward the center of the road or an approaching vehicle to enable the driver to see the vehicle behind him better.

Cf. fishtail.

lay on the air: to apply the brakes.

Syn.: set her down, spike it, throw out the anchor.

lay over: **1.** to take a rest of eight or more hours, before continuing a trip, a legal requirement if driving for ten previous hours. A trucker may also lay over if he waits overnight to make a delivery in the morning.

2. The money a trucker is paid by his company for making a lay over (usually to insure first-thing-in-the-morning delivery).

Cf. shut out.

lead driver: the senior or first driver of a two-man team.

Cf. concentrator, copilot, divorced, married, navigator, ride shotgun, second driver.

lead foot: **1.** a trucker who drives at or near top speed. **2.** Said to be possessed by a trucker who drives fast.

Syn.: aviator, highballer.

Cf. big hole it, floorboard it.

lean on it: to drive a truck at high speed.

Syn.: big hole it, burn the breeze, floorboard it, run wide open, turn it on.

leapin' Lena: a lightweight truck.

Syn.: candy wagon, puddle jumper.

Cf. bundle buggy, straight job.

level deck lowboy: a lowboy trailer that has a one-level bed behind the gooseneck, as opposed to a double-drop lowboy.

Cf. detachable gooseneck, double-drop trailer, gooseneck, stretch lowboy, swing brackets.

leveling block: used with a single-drop trailer, the triangular-shaped wooden wedge that serves to support cargo placed on the raised part of the deck and extends beyond the drop. The leveling block is the width of the trailer (eight feet) and the height of the drop in the trailer's deck (usually one foot).
Cf. single-drop trailer.

lie sheet: a driver's log book.
Syn.: swindle sheet.
Cf. log book.

line: a road, route or highway.
Cf. berm, lane hopper, holy road, pike, spooks, tied up.

line driver: an over-the-road driver.
Syn.: big rig man, gear shifter, long-haul driver, semi driver.

line haul: a scheduled truck run or movement of freight between cities.
Cf. flyer, hot load, peddle run, pension run, relay.

line-haul driver: a trucker who has a regularly scheduled truck run.
Cf. line driver, long-haul driver.

live axle: an axle that transmits power and is not present on the tractor merely to raise the weight allowance of the rig.
Syn.: drive axle.
Cf. axle, bogies, dead axle, full screw, steering axle, trail axle.

livestock body: a trailer designed for transporting

cattle, hogs, sheep, horses or other farm animals.
Cf. bull rack, possum belly.

load her heavy on the high side: to load cargo toward the left side of a trailer in order to carry most of the weight on the higher side of the road and because the load will shift slightly to the right during transport.
Cf. button her up, clamp on the binders.

load of postholes: what a trucker hauls when he has no cargo.
Syn.: deadhead haul.
Cf. hauling postholes.

load of sand: a cargo of sugar.
Syn.: crate of sand.
Cf. load of suds, load of wind.

load of suds: a cargo of beer.
Cf. load of postholes, load of sand, zephyr haul.

load of wind: a shipment of light but bulky cargo.
Syn.: balloon freight, zephyr haul.
Cf. swinger.

log book: the daily log in which truckers list their activities including driving time, on duty—not driving time, off-duty time, bunk time, layovers, deliveries, pickups, mileage, the truck's condition and performance, and part replacement, if any. The I.C.C. requires that an accurate and up-to-date log be kept by all truckers unless they operate within a fifty-mile radius of their home terminal and use a time clock. The log is always subject to inspection by officials.
Syn.: lie sheet, swindle sheet.

Cf. V.C.R.

log bunks: metal bars that are thirty-six inches or more in length and form a U-shaped receptacle on a pole trailer to keep logs from rolling.
Cf. cant hook, pole trailer, stick hauler.

long double: a double-bottom combination that uses two full-length trailers.
Syn.: train.
Cf. centipede, dual shorts, rolling doughnuts, semi and pup, short bottom, trainman's license.

long-haul driver: a trucker who specializes in long-distance driving.
Syn.: line driver, over-the-road driver.

long logger: a straight job with a log trailer hitched on behind; logs are carried on both truck and trailer.
Cf. muley cow, pole trailer, stick hauler.

long-nose: describes a conventional cab with a long hood.
Cf. bonnet, short-nose, whalenose.

look-see window: a window in the rear of the sleeper that assists the driver in backing up by increasing his visibility.
Cf. picture windows, sleeperette.

loose horse: a tractor without its semi-trailer.
Syn.: bareback, bobtail, solo.
Cf. bobtail miles, horse.

loping: variation in an engine's revolutions per minute while it is idling.
Syn.: galloping, hunting.

low-air warning device: any mechanical means of notifying a truck driver that his vehicle is not maintaining the proper amount of air pressure, which is needed to operate the brakes, windshield wipers, shutterstat and some transmissions. Every truck carries two of the following low-air warning devices: a buzzer, a flashing red light on the instrument panel, a small red metal flag that drops into the driver's line of vision.

Cf. breakaway valve, four-way relay emergency valve, spit valve.

lowboy: a sideless trailer set low to the ground and usually used to transport exceptionally high cargo or construction or farm equipment and machinery.

Cf. detachable gooseneck, double-drop trailer, expandable lowboy, gooseneck lowboy, level deck lowboy, outriggers.

low side: the lower speed in a two-speed auxiliary transmission.

Cf. duplex, high side, high split, low split, overdrive, two-way split.

low split: the low side of a three-speed auxiliary transmission.

Cf. high split, three-way split, triplex.

L.T.L.: refers to cargo shipments of less than truckload size and weight; usually handled at proportionately higher rates and freight charges.

Syn.: part load.

Cf. bill of lading, free astray, minnie, tariff.

luberfiner: an oil purifier attached to the outside of an engine. Presumably, the term is a blend made from "lubricant refiner."

lugging: driving a rig in a higher gear range than the engine's revolutions per minute require for the work at hand. The driver should downgear to save his equipment from excessive wear and strain.

Syn.: drag down.

Cf. back off, drop gears, feather, grab one, keep 'er winding, overspeed, tachometer, windmill.

lunette: the steel ring to which the pintle assembly is hooked in order to tow a full trailer.

Cf. double-bottom rig, full trailer, tongue, truck-trailer, whippletree.

M

Mack: a popular, economical and long-wearing make of tractor, the one best known to the public. Like the GMC, the Mack engine has a characteristic sound, a husky growl. The Mack trademark is a bulldog, and every tractor has a replica above the grill. For that reason, it is said that a trucker who wheels a Mack "follows the bulldog." The transmission names duplex (five-by-two), triplex (five-by-three) and quadriplex (five-by-four) are synonymous with Mack. All of these transmissions have two gearshift levers on one gearbox; they are to be carefully differentiated from transmissions with two gear boxes.

Syn.: bull dog.

Cf. anteater, bark, B-model, cherry picker, sidewinder, unishift.

mag brake: a brake shoe made of a steel and magnesium alloy; popular in the mountainous west because the hotter a mag becomes the better it holds.

Syn.: hot foot, hot shoe, steely.

Cf. pancake.

main box: the main gearbox, which determines the speed of a tractor. It generally has four or five gears plus one reverse gear. It may be used with an auxiliary transmission with two, three or four gears; it may also be coupled with a two- or three-speed rear end assembly.

Cf. aux box, brownie, gearboxes, Roadranger, Spicer, two-way split, three-way split, two-stick transmission, unishift.

make some miles: to drive a truck.

Syn.: eatin' concrete, grab some gears, push a rig.

maniac: a shop mechanic.

Syn.: hood lifter.

Cf. chief hood lifter, grease monkey, ice man, sledgehammer mechanic.

manure-spreader wheels: spoke wheels on a truck; so named because they largely resemble those used on manure spreaders.

Syn.: Dayton wheels, square wheels, wobblers.

Cf. Budd wheels, babymoon hubcaps.

marker lights: the small lights that serve to outline a truck's length and width at night and in bad weather. Lights on the front and side are amber; those at the rear are red.

Syn.: clearance lights, running lights.

Cf. bus markers, identification lights, torpedoes, use the feelers.

married: refers to the drivers in a two-man operation or driving team.

Cf. divorced, lead driver, ride shotgun, roving team, run double, swamper.

matchbox Jimmy: the cabover tractor that was manufactured by General Motors up until a few years ago; so named because of its boxlike appearance.

Syn.: crackerbox Jimmy.

Cf. Detroit Diesel, Hillbilly Special, Jamie, poor man's tractor.

meat hauler: a trucker who hauls swinging beef or processed meat, as opposed to a bull hauler, who transports the beef on the hoof.

Cf. hog hauler, railer, swingin' beef.

mechanized cow: a tractor-trailer with a bulk milk tank.

Cf. tanker.

Mexican Freightliner: the model 5000 White tractor; by implication of the nickname, a bargain-basement version of the White Freightliner. This tractor gained its nickname because the cab is made completely of fiberglass.

Syn.: Japanese Freightliner.

Cf. Fruitliner.

Mexican overdrive: the "gear" a trucker uses when, in going downhill, he throws the transmission out of gear and lets the truck coast down in neutral.

Syn.: eleventh gear, Georgia overdrive, Jewish overdrive, midnight overdrive, thirteenth gear.

Cf. wobbly hole.

Note: Allowing a truck to coast down hill is illegal and can harm the transmission.

Michigan rig: a double-bottom rig out of Michigan, where such combinations are legal; it is characterized by the number of its axles, anywhere from eight to thirteen, as opposed to the usual tractor-trailer combination of from three to six axles. A typical Michigan rig might be composed of a tandem-axle tractor, a four-axle trailer, a converter dolly with two axles, and a second trailer with three axles (twelve axles altogether).

Syn.: rolling doughnuts.

Cf. centipede, dual shorts, long double, set of joints, short bottom, trainman's license.

Michigan spread: a trailer with a separation of nine feet between the two axles.

Cf. Ohio spread, spread, tandem spread, three-legged trailer, three nines, wide-spread.

micks: Michelin tires.

Cf. baloneys, California tires, Pennsylvania caps, rider, rubber, singing, waffles.

midnight overdrive: the "gear" a trucker uses when, in traveling downhill, he throws the transmission out of gear and lets the truck coast down in neutral (an illegal practice).

Syn.: eleventh gear, Georgia overdrive, Jewish overdrive, Mexican overdrive, thirteenth gear.

milk run: an easy trip.

Cf. gravy hauler.

mill: the engine in a tractor. It is with pride that a trucker speaks of the many horses his mill produces.

Syn.: power plant.

Cf. horse.

milograph: the gauge that contains the odometer and speedometer.

Cf. hub-o-meter, tachometer, tattletale.

minnie: any small freight shipment that is shipped at the minimum freight rate.

Cf. bill of lading, I.C.C., L.T.L., tariff.

miss a hole: to fail to get the gearshift into the desired position when changing gears. It is not hard to do; even experts miss occasionally.

Cf. scratch one in, split the cogs.

mixed truckload: one shipment composed of different commodities.

Cf. feeder service, free astray.

mixer: a truck with a cement mixer body used to transport intransit mixed cement to a building site.

Cf. front PTO, hot mix.

mixing stick: the gearshift lever.

Syn.: wobblestick.

Cf. mix-master special.

mix-master special: any transmission with two shift levers; so named because, in running through the gears, the trucker's hands are constantly in motion.

Syn.: two-stick transmission.

Cf. aux box, duplex, main box, quad, triplex.

moisture-release valve: a valve in the air line that emits some air each time the brakes of the tractor are applied. It prevents water and moisture from collecting in the air system.

Syn.: spit valve.

Cf. air brakes, bleed the tir tanks, low-air warning device.

moneymaker: any low-priced, dependable tractor.
Syn.: tightwad tractor.
Cf. poor man's tractor, turnpike tightwad.

monkey bar: the hand valve that controls trailer brake application and is usually mounted on the steering column. It may be used independently to apply only the trailer brakes or as a supplement to the foot-brake system, which applies the brakes equally in tractor and trailer.
Syn.: hand valve, trolley-valve handle.
Cf. four-way relay emergency valve, Johnson bar, tractor-protection valve.

moonlight: to haul illegal commodities or to backhaul a commodity without having authority from the Interstate Commerce Commission.
Cf. boondockin', grandfather rights, hot load, Moonlight Express, run legal, runnin' hot, tariff, wildcatter.

moonlighter: a trucker who hauls freight without authority; so named because he usually runs only at night to avoid detection.
Syn.: gypsy, wildcatter.
Cf. four-laner, Moonlight Express, runnin' hot.

Moonlight Express: the "company," not sanctioned by the I.C.C. and consequently illegal, that hauls a sizable percentage (approximately 10 percent) of the motor carrier freight in the nation. The "Express" has no published tariffs and therefore no uniform pay scale. Some shippers are glad to use the Moonlight Express because of its usually rapid and efficient transportation of goods and materials.
Cf. boondockin', hot load, runnin' hot, wildcat.

mothballs: balls of ether used by truckers to start cold diesel engines.
Syn.: gumballs.
Cf. ether lock, summertime truck.

mountain climbin' job: the task of a household goods mover when he must carry the furniture out to the truck from a second- or third-story dwelling.
Cf. bedbug hauler.

muck hauler: a trucker who hauls phosphate from a mine to a plant for refining.

mud flaps: large rubber or metal flaps hung behind the tires of a tractor-trailer that protect it and vehicles following it from the snow, mud or rocks that its tires might kick up.
Cf. antifly device, shroud.

mud season: the early spring thaw, which generally brings to a halt off-the-road trucking operations. Some states even lower the axle weight and gross weight they permit on their roads during the mud season.

mud trailer: a flat bed trailer that has a unique device to facilitate cargo loading. Before the tractor is hooked up, the dollies retract, lowering the nose of the flat to the ground. The cargo is then loaded by being slid up the lowered end. The flat is raised by means of a winch mounted on the rear of the tractor for this purpose.
Syn.: float.
Cf. drop it on the nose, winch rig.

mule: a small tractor used to relocate dollies in a terminal or warehouse.
Syn.: doodle-bug.

Cf. yard bird, yard mule.

muley cow: a long pole with a spiked end and a steel hook that is used by loggers and by truckers who drive logging rigs to turn logs over.

Syn.: cant hook.

Cf. pole trailer, stick hauler.

multistop run: a run on which the driver makes frequent stops to deliver goods.

Syn.: peddle run.

Cf. sprinkle a load, string it.

N

nameplate finders: cab-mounted spotlights used to find an address on a building at night.

Syn.: house number hunters.

Cf. coon light, dual spots, horse light.

navigator: the co-driver of a two-man operation who reads the road maps while going through unfamiliar towns.

Cf. concentrator, married.

need a hinge: a truck needs a "hinge" when a corner to be negotiated is too sharp.

Cf. chop a turn, split-arc, wrap 'er around the bend.

noisemaker: a radio in a truck.

Syn.: hillbilly operahouse, fiddle.

Cf. butt kit, stove and fiddle.

nose: the foremost part of a trailer.

Cf. bulkhead, dollies, drop it on the nose.

nose dive: refers to a trailer that has tipped forward on its nose when dropped or parked by the driver.

Cf. drop it on the nose.

number-one hole: the gearshift position for the lowest combination of gears in a transmission.

Syn.: creeper gear, down in the corner, grandma gear, growler, ought hole.

Cf. big hole, pay hole, whistlin' gear.

O

oakie blower: an air scoop on the air-intake system of an engine that increases engine power.

Cf. blower, gutless wonder, horses, husky oat motor, supercharger, turbocharger.

odometer: an instrument that measures the total number of miles traveled by a vehicle.

Cf. hub-o-meter, milograph, tattletale.

Ohio spread: a trailer with a separation of eight feet between the axles.

Cf. Michigan spread, spread, three-legged trailer, wide-spread.

oil burner: **1.** a diesel truck, as opposed to a truck that runs on gasoline.

Syn.: diesel, smoker.

Cf. bubble burner, banger, four-lunger, gas job, juice jockey.

2. a truck whose engine uses a great deal of oil.

Cf. working for Standard Oil.

oil field body: a platform trailer equipped with instruments for oil drilling.

Syn.: oil field float.

Cf. gin poles.

oil field float: a platform trailer specially equipped for oil field work.

Syn.: oil field body.

oil field hauler: a specialized carrier of oil field equipment.

Cf. specialized carrier.

oil gauge: the gauge on a tractor's dash that shows the trucker the oil pressure in the engine.

Cf. idiot light, working for Standard Oil.

on behind: refers to the payload on a trailer (as in "I pulled Chicago with forty thousand pounds on behind").

Cf. curb weight, gross weight.

open 'er up: **1.** to run a truck at full speed.

Syn.: big hole it, flying low, haul the mail, tacked out, turn it on.

2. to turn the engine governor up to increase the revolutions per minute.

Cf. governor.

3. to increase the fuel portion in the fuel-to-air ratio in the cylinders.

Syn.: set it up, turn the wick up.

Cf. cut 'er down, weaned out.

open top: **1.** a van with an open top; usually covered over with a tarp to prevent weather damage to the cargo.

Cf. circus wagon, header bar, rag top.

2. a flat bed trailer with removable high sides but no permanent top; used primarily for hauling heavy machinery, which is lowered into place with a crane, or for hauling stone or gravel.

Syn.: converto-van.

Cf. button her up.

ought hole: the gearshift position for the lowest combination of gears in a tractor.

Syn.: grandma gear, growler, number-one hole.

Cf. midnight overdrive, pay hole, whistlin' gear.

out of service: **1.** a driver who is off duty. **2.** a truck, tractor or trailer that has failed to pass the mandatory I.C.C. safety inspection is placed "out of service" until it can pass.

Cf. grounded.

outriggers: the short brackets that extend, if needed, from the sides of a lowboy trailer. Should the payload be wider than the trailer, planks are run across the tops of the outriggers to receive the additional width.

Syn.: swing brackets.

Cf. detachable gooseneck, expandable lowboy, well.

overage: freight in excess of the quantity believed to have been shipped or of the amount shown on the bill of lading.

Cf. claim, shortage.

over and under: an auxiliary transmission.

Cf. brownie, quad, three-way split, triplex.

overdimensional load: any load that exceeds the legal size and weight limits of the state through which the tractor-trailer is traveling.

Cf. boondockin', eyeball it, I.C.C., permit, pretties, P.U.C., runnin' hot.

overdrive: **1.** the highest gear of any transmission; used for hauling light loads and for deadheading because the engine turns slower than the drive line when the transmission is in overdrive. It slows the engine's revolutions per minute for the purpose of economy and makes possible a higher top speed with a lower rear end ratio.

Cf. double overdrive, Georgia overdrive.

2. "Overdrive" is the monthly truckers' magazine, champion of the owner-operator and the small trucker.

over on the drive: the condition in which too much of a rig's weight rests on the drive axle of the tractor.

Cf. axle out a load, axle weight, curb weight, gross weight.

overspeed: to run an engine at an excessive number of revolutions per minute for the gear being used. The driver should shift to a higher gear to save the engine from wear.

Syn.: can the motor.

Cf. back off, keep 'er winding, lugging, tachometer, windmill.

over-the-road driver: a driver who hauls goods long distances or one who may make a trip of two or more day's duration.

Syn.: line driver, long-haul driver.

Cf. trucker.

owner-operator: a trucker who both owns and drives his rig.

Cf. broker, cardboard driver, free passes to bankruptcy, gypsy, trip lease, wildcat.

P

painted scrap-iron hauler: a trucker who transports knock-down farm machinery such as that manufactured by John Deere, Allis-Chalmers, Oliver Corporation and International Harvester.
Cf. heavy hauler, iron hauler.

pajama wagon: any conventional cab with a factory-built sleeping compartment as opposed to a conventional with a suicide box.
Cf. coffin box, pull a sleep job, roll and rest, slumber slot, vanliner.

pallet: a small wooden skid or platform on which material is stacked and which is moved or loaded onto a trailer by means of a fork lift.
Cf. dock monkey, fork lift.

pancake: an air brake diaphragm that activates the brake cylinder.
Cf. air brakes, mag brake, sucker brake.

panel body: a small enclosed truck used for delivering packages.
Cf. bundle buggy.

part load: a consignment to a destination that is less than a complete trailer load.
Syn.: L.T.L., minnie.
Cf. free astray, mixed truckload, swinger.

pay hole: a truck's highest gear.
Syn.: go-away gear, goin' home hole, whistlin' gear.
Cf. hook 'er into high, overdrive, tacked out.

pay load: the cargo or freight that a trucker hauls.
Cf. clock load, hot load, load of postholes, load of suds, red label load, zephyr haul.

peach picker: a high cabover tractor; probably first named by a short trucker who found the climb to the driver's seat strenuous.
Syn.: cherry picker.

peanut roaster: an intake manifold with a leak.
Cf. punctured lung, ventilate the motor.

peanut wagon: any small tractor pulling a large trailer.
Cf. drag, gutless wonder, rinky dink.

peddle run: a truck run with frequent deliveries, as opposed to a run with only one destination.
Syn.: multistop run.
Cf. chimney sweep run, sprinkle a load, string it.

peek-a-boo mirrors: small, round convex mirrors on a tractor.
Syn.: powderpuff, spot mirror.
Cf. cop spotter, Volkswagen spotter, West Coast mirrors.

peel out: to make a fast start.
Syn.: dig out.
Cf. running start

peg leg: **1.** the first rear axle of a tandem-axle tractor when it has only single tires.
Syn.: half axle.
Cf. floats.
2. a three-legged trailer, which is a triaxle trailer with a nine-foot separation between the second and third axles.
3. a trailer with one broken dolly or that lacks a footpad or wheels to the landing gear assembly.

Pennsylvania caps: recapped tires with an unbroken tread line; such tires create a good deal of road noise.

Syn.: cop callers, singers.

Cf. California tires, full cap, micks, singing, surface cap.

pension run: an easy, regular run.

Syn.: milk run.

Cf. clock load.

percolator: the carburetor.

Syn.: juice pot.

Cf. bubble burner, diesel, gas job, juice jockey, oil burner.

permit: written permission obtained by a company from a state that allows the passage of an overdimensional load. A permit usually specifies the date of the haul, the routes to be covered, the name of the driver, the year, make and serial numbers of the tractor and the trailer, the nature of the commodity and the feature that makes the load overdimensional (e.g., a height of 13′10″, a width of 9′3″ or a gross weight of eighty thousand pounds).

Cf. overdimensional load, pretties, P.U.C., runnin' hot.

Pete: short for Peterbilt, one of the most luxurious makes of tractors manufactured and a close competitor with Kenworth tractors in both cost and quality.

Cf. rolling palace, vanliner.

picture windows: windows around the sides and rear of an Emeryville tractor that is not designed to have a sleeper.

Cf. look-see window, sleeperette.

pig: 1. the complete gear setup of a tractor's rear end; it serves to redirect the power from the drive shaft to the wheels.
Cf. banjo, rear end assembly.
2. a sloppy waitress in a truck stop.
Cf. pigsty.
3. a trailer that is transported on a railroad flat car.
Cf. piggybacking.

piggybacking: the practice of shipping loaded trailers or automobiles on railroad flat cars, a potential threat to the livelihood of truckers.
Cf. birdyback, containerization, fishyback.

Pig Iron Express: the mythical "company" to which a steel division driver for Pacific Intermountain Express belongs. If a driver stated that he drove for Pig Iron Express, you would know that he was referring to P.I.E.'s steel division.
Cf. iron hauler, painted scrap-iron hauler, Pork Chop Express.

pigpen: a sloppy, ill-run truck stop.
Syn.: choke and puke, greasy spoon, pigsty.
Cf. pig, fuel stop, truck stop.

pigsty: a sloppy, ill-run truck stop.
Syn.: pigpen.
Cf. pig.

pigtail: the cable that transmits electricity to the trailer from the tractor.
Syn: trolley wire.
Cf. air hose, glad hand, pogo stick, trailer connections.

pike: any turnpike.
Cf. berm, line, religious road, spooks, tied up.

pile up: to wreck a truck.
Cf. belly up, buy up an orchard, jackknife, tailgating, total it out.

pin: the heavy-duty coupling beneath the nose of a semi-trailer that is locked into the fifth wheel of a tractor when a trucker hooks up.
Syn.: kingpin.
Cf. air slider, cup and saucer, fifth wheel, jump the pin, pull the pin.

pin setting: the placement of the kingpin beneath the trailer's nose; it ranges from eighteen to forty-eight inches from the front of the semi. Different pin locations can change the amount of load that bears on the drive and steering axles of the tractor, and also the overall length of the combination. Some trailers have two pins so that they can conform to the various regulations applied to load and length requirements in cross-continental transportation.
Cf. kingpin.

pintle hook: a hooking device seen on oil field rigs and used to couple a full trailer to a truck or to pull a semi-trailer onto a fifth wheel.
Cf. lunette.

platform: a flat bed trailer, a trailer that has a deck (or platform) on which cargo rests but no sides.
Syn.: flat bed, flat bottom, flat deck.
Cf. convertible, rub rails, single-drop trailer, stretch flat.

pneumonia sedan: a truck with no window glass.
Cf. eskimo, sweat shop.

pogo stick: a projection on the rear of a tractor that keeps the air lines and the electric cable from dragging between the tractor and the trailer.
Syn.: hitchhiker.
Cf. pigtail, trolley lines.

point of origin: the collecting terminal at which freight is received from various shippers for a long run to another region.
Cf. feeder service, initial carrier.

pole trailer: a trailer composed of a single telescopic pole, a tandem rear-wheel unit and a coupling device used to join the trailer to a tractor. Pole trailers are used to transport logs or any long freight, which is lashed to the central supporting pole and thereby serves as its own trailer. Pole trailers are adjustable in length in much the same manner as sliding curtain rods.
Cf. expandable lowboy, muley cow, short couple, short logger, stick hauler, stretch flat.

pony wheels: an extra set of wheels located behind the drive axle on a straight job that are usually used in hauling logs. When the vehicle is empty, the extra wheels clear the ground; when it is loaded, they rest on the ground.
Syn.: donkey wheels.
Cf. cheater axle.

poor man's tractor: any tractor manufactured by General Motors Corporation or any truck with a Detroit diesel engine.
Syn.: Hillbilly Special, Jimmy, screamin' Lena.
Cf. moneymaker, tightwad tractor.

Pork Chop Express: the imaginary, collective "company" of all hog haulers.
Syn.: shoat and goat conductor.
Cf. bull hauler, cackle crate, possum belly, shoat boat.

possum belly: a double-deck livestock trailer that can carry at least forty head of cattle. If the animals are of a short-legged breed, or are hogs, sheep or calves, the trailer can be converted to three or more levels. The name is derived from the drop frame of the trailer, which is only inches above the ground.
Syn.: pot belly.
Cf. bull rack, drop bottom, shoat boat.

postage stamp: state permits in the form of small decals that must be placed on a tractor so that it may regularly pass through the issuing state.
Syn.: pretties.
Cf. permit.

pot: the housing in the rear axles that holds the differential, the ring gear and the pinion gear. This rear end assembly serves to redirect the power from the drive shaft to the rear wheels.
Syn.: banjo.
Cf. pig, rear end assembly.

pot belly: a trailer with a drop frame that is used for hauling livestock.
Syn.: possum belly.
Cf. bull rack.

pots: pot torches placed on a highway to warn traffic of an obstruction or hazard. The I.C.C. requires all truckers to carry safety equipment (red flags, red reflectors, pot torches or fuses) to be set out in case of an accident involving themselves or others.

Cf. candles.

pour it on: to drive fast.

Syn.: big hole it, pour on the coals.

Cf. foot in the floorboards, haul the mail, tacked out.

pour on the coals: to drive a truck at high speed.

Syn.: floorboard it, lean on it, run wide open.

powderpuff: a small convex mirror on a tractor.

Syn.: peek-a-boo mirrors, spot mirror.

Cf. West Coast mirrors.

power: the tractor; short for "power unit."

Syn.: horse, unit.

powered by rubber bands: said of a tractor that has a tag axle run by V-belts, which transmit power from the drive axle.

Cf. belt drive, cheater axle, dead axle, rubber band drive.

power lift gate: a power gate on the rear of some straight trucks that is used to lift heavy loads up to floor level; usually electrically or hydraulically powered.

Syn.: elevator.

power plant: a tractor's engine, usually of a high horsepower rating.

Syn.: mill.

Cf. dog catcher.

pretties: permanent state permits in the form of small decals that must be placed on a tractor.

Syn.: postage stamps.

Cf. permit.

private carrier: a firm which maintains trucks to ship its own raw materials or finished products; transportation is incidental to the company's main business activity.

Cf. carrier, common carrier, for-hire carrier, exempt carrier.

produce hauler: a trucker who transports fruits, vegetables and other produce.

Syn.: garbage hauler.

Cf. bean hauler, gravy hauler, green stuff, iron hauler, meat hauler, shoat and goat conductor, weeder geese hauler.

progressive: said of a transmission that has an even r.p.m. split between gears, it "progresses evenly." An example is the five-and-two direct transmission.

Cf. idiot transmission.

P.U.C.: the Public Utilities Commission, which frequently stops trucks to check bills of lading and company authority.

Cf. boondockin', **D**eath **o**n **T**ruckers, decals, I.C.C., pretties, tariff, wildcatter.

puddle jumper: a lightweight truck.

Syn.: candy wagon.

Cf. bundle buggy, tap dancer.

pug: a cabover tractor.

Syn.: blunt-nose, flat face, snub-nose.

Cf. conventional cab, flip top.

pull: to drive a truck to a specific town or location. ("I pulled St. Louis twice last week.")

Cf. turn.

pull a sleep job: to drive a semi into a service plaza or rest area or onto the shoulder of the road in order to take a rest.

Cf. bedsteader, eye trouble, roll and rest.

pulling gear: the gear in which a truck can climb a

hill. While ascending any grade, a trucker downshifts until he reaches the gear in which his truck will maintain its speed and power to the top of the hill.

Cf. big hole, gettin' stretched, grab a gear, grandma gear, tacked out.

pull into: to arrive at (a particular place or destination).

Cf. pull, turn.

pullman: a trailer adapted for the transportation of livestock, usually horses or cattle.

Syn.: bull rack.

Cf. pot belly, shoat boat.

pull one's decals: to remove a company's decals from the doors of a tractor; usually done by an owner-operator when he leaves the company.

Cf. cardboard driver, decals, pretties.

pull the pin: to release the lock holding a semi-trailer to the fifth wheel of a tractor.

Syn.: unlatch.

Cf. break the unit, drop it on the nose, jump the pin, kingpin, pin setting.

pumpkin: a flat tire.

Syn.: rider.

Cf. cheater slicks, duals, dusting, ride a fire-bug.

punctured lung: a leaky radiator in a rig.

Cf. water dog, slop the hogs.

pup: any four-wheel trailer, characterized by its short wheel base. A pup trailer may be used as the second unit in a truck-trailer combination or in a semi and pup combination.

Syn.: four-wheeler, kite.

Cf. blimp, deck and four-wheeler, dual shorts, short bottom.

push a rig: to drive a truck.

Syn.: wheel a rig.

Cf. eatin' concrete, grab some gears, make some miles.

pusher: **1.** the rearmost axle of a tandem-axle tractor is known as a pusher if it is a drive axle and the axle located in front of it is a dead axle.

Cf. live axle, spider, trail axle.

2. a company employee who hurries the loading and unloading of trucks at a dock.

Syn.: chaser.

Cf. dock walloper, swamper.

push 'n' wonder brakes: the vacuum-over-hydraulic system found on old-time tractor-trailers, a system whose efficiency was so erratic that a driver would push on the brake pedal and wonder if he would stop.

Cf. singer, slave ship, sucker brake.

put on the air: to apply the brakes.

Syn: clamp on the binders, grab some air, lay on the air, set her down, throw out the anchor.

put on the iron: to put on tire chains.

Cf. irons, sanders, waffles.

put to sleep: describes a company man who has run his full time allotment for driving and is given eight hours of off-duty time (by I.C.C. regulations) in which to rest before making another run. He is usually put to sleep at a company terminal; if he is on the road and has used up his driving time, he is supposed to lay over for the eight hours.

Cf. lay over, pull a sleep job, roll and rest.

putt-putt: a one-cylinder gas engine used to power the blower of a bunker and the blower unit on a refrigerated trailer.

Cf. bunker, cold blow, ice man, reefer.

pyrometer: the heat gauge for an exhaust stack that indicates the temperature of the exhaust.

Cf. smokestack.

Q

quad: **1.** a Mack transmission that has two sticks on one gearbox. Short for quadriplex, the quad is a twenty-speed (five-by-four) transmission.

Cf. duplex, triplex, unishift.

2. the Spicer four-by-four transmission.

Cf. four-way split, gearboxes, mix-master special, Spicer.

quadriplex: a Mack transmission having five speeds controlled by the main gearshift and four speeds controlled by the auxiliary gearshift; it has a total of twenty forward speeds and four reverse speeds.

Syn.: quad.

Cf. duplex, Mack, triplex, unishift.

quick-disconnect couplers: fittings for air or hydraulic hoses that enable them to be easily connected and disconnected. They usually are equipped with automatic valves that shut off the flow of air or liquid from each half when disconnected.

Cf. trailer connections.

R

racin' slicks: badly worn-out tires.

Syn.: California tires, cheater slicks, rags.

Cf. pumpkin, rider, rubber, tire billy.

Radar Alley: Interstate 90, between Cleveland and the New York line; so named because of the numerous radar traps set on the road.

Cf. big hat, bird dog, bubble gum machine, vulture.

rags: bad tires.

Syn.: California tires, cheater slicks, racin' slicks.

Cf. kick the doughnuts, pumpkin rider, tire billy.

rag top: **1.** a low-sided trailer with metal bows over the top to support a tarpaulin.

Syn.: circus wagon.

Cf. button her up.

2. an open top van with a tarpaulin covering over the top.

Cf. converto-van, open top.

railer: a reefer with a rail or track assembly used for hauling fresh meat sides and quarters, which are suspended from the roof.

Cf. cold box, meat hauler, swingin' beef.

rate: the charge for transporting freight.

Cf. bill of lading, minnie, L.T.L., tariff.

rat race: four or five trucks running down the road in a group.
Cf. convoy, family reunion, stay on his tail.

reach: the telescoping pole on a pole trailer that connects the wheel assembly of the trailer to a tractor.
Cf. cant hook, pole trailer, short couple, short logger, stick hauler, stinger.

reach for the air: to apply the brakes.
Syn.: grab a handful of air, set her down, spike it.
Cf. emerjensen, trolley-valve handle.

real amateur: a careless driver.
Cf. cowboy, road hog, Sears-Roebuck license, tailboard artist.

rear dump: a trailer that can be tilted to unload the cargo through a rear gate.
Syn.; dump body, tipper.
Cf. bottom dumps, hopper body.

rear end assembly: the complete gear setup that serves to redirect the power from the tractor's drive shaft to the wheels.
Cf. banjo, pig, pot.

red label load: a cargo of flammable or explosive goods.
Cf. boom wagon, dangerous articles, suicide jockey, widow-maker.

Redwood Tree: the air-intake stack on a Peterbilt tractor; it can be mounted outside the cab on special order, but on standard Peterbilts it runs through the luggage compartment and sleeper on the co-driver's side, is unsightly and takes up valuable space.
Cf. bonnet, breather.

reefer: a refrigerated trailer.
Syn.: cold box, ice box, ice wagon.
Cf. bunker, cold blow, dry box, ice man, insulated body, putt-putt, railer.

rehaul: to go over a truck; the word is a blend of "repair" and "overhaul."
Cf. broke to lead, cut her water off and read her meter.

relay: a procedure commonly used in companies to keep as many trucks as possible moving over the road. In one kind of relay, different truckers drive the same rig toward an ultimate destination. In another type of relay, a trucker runs to an agreed switching point, where he exchanges rigs with another driver from his company, returning to his original terminal or departure point with the second truck. Meanwhile, the second driver returns to his terminal with the first man's rig. In this way, each driver runs his allotted road time, the freight is delivered, and each driver has the advantage of covering routes that he knows thoroughly. The nature of a relay is often expressed according to the number of hours of road time per driver; for instance, in a "five-hour relay" the drivers change every five hours.
Cf. bid run, clock run, milk run, peddle run, roster, roving team, slip-seat operation.

religious road: a broken-up highway with many potholes.
Syn.: holy road.
Cf. berm, line, religious states, spooks, pike.

religious states: states that do not clear snow from their highways (their philosophy is "If God put the snow there, let Him take it away" truckers presume).

Cf. holy road.

religious tarps: tarpaulins with many tears and holes in them.

Syn.: sunshine tarps.

relocation consultant: a trucker who drives a moving van.

Syn.: bedbug hauler.

Cf. commercial highway engineer, distribution technician, household goods hauler, mountain climbin' job.

removable kingpin: **1.** a kingpin on a trailer that can be removed and placed in a second pin setting.

Cf. pin setting, pull the pin, unlatch.

2. a fifth wheel kingpin on an oil field truck used to receive the inverted fifth wheel of a trailer.

Cf. cup and saucer, inverted fifth wheel.

residenter: any old tractor still used over the road.

Cf. been around the horn, junker.

rev: to speed up (an engine).

rib-side: describes a box trailer whose side ridges are vertical to the ground, resembling ribs.

Cf. corrugated, smooth-side.

ride a firebug: to drive a truck with a flat dual wheel tire, which is a fire hazard.

Cf. dusting, rags, pumpkin, rider, tire billy.

rider: a flat tire on a set of duals. Since it carries none of the weight of the load, a rider throws additional strain on the remaining good tire, thereby increasing the probability of its having a blowout.

Syn.: pumpkin.

Cf. kick the doughnuts, ride a firebug, tire billy.

ride shotgun: to ride in the passenger seat of the tractor.

Cf. lead driver, run double, second driver, shotgun, swamper.

rig: a truck; any tractor-trailer combination.

Syn.: big rig, combination, diesel, semi, tandem, widow-maker.

Cf. big rig man.

rinky dink: the model 4000 White tractor, which is a small conventional cab without a sleeper.

Cf. bubble-nose White, Mexican Freightliner, pajama wagon.

road bum: any unsavory looking trucker.

Cf. truck-stop commando.

Roadeo: the National Truck Roadeo, an exhibition and competition of driving skills in various classifications of motor vehicles for expert truckers. Sponsored annually by the American Trucking Association, it serves to recognize the best and safest professional drivers. Grading is based on (1) appearance, (2) knowledge displayed on written tests of safe-driving rules, the trucking industry, first aid and fire-fighting and (3) driving-skill field tests.

road hog: a motorist who takes his half of the road out of the middle.

Cf. eight-miler, lane hopper, real amateur.

Roadranger: a Fuller transmission with one gear stick. After the trucker runs through the first round of gears (the low side), he pulls a lever on the gear shift, moves it back to the starting position, and runs through the shifting pattern a second time to get the higher gears. A Roadranger has from eight to thirteen speeds and is always used with a single-speed rear axle.

Cf. deep-reduction valve, searcher, splitter.

rock it: to free a vehicle from mud or snow by first driving forward and then driving in reverse.

Cf. frogging, tow hooks.

roll and rest: to alternately drive and stop to sleep at planned intervals.

Cf. bedsteader, eye trouble, pull a sleep job.

rolling doughnuts: a double-bottom rig wth ten or more axles.

Syn.: Michigan rig.

Cf. centipede, dual shorts, long double.

rolling lighthouse: a tractor-trailer with more than the customary number of clearance and fog lights.

Syn.: Christmas tree.

Cf.: rolling palace.

rolling palace: any luxurious tractor, usually an owner-operator's pride and joy, as opposed to the minimal sort of rigs many companies have. It can be any make of tractor but is most commonly a Peterbilt, White Freightliner or Kenworth. The extras may include a custom paint job, plenty of chrome trim (stacks, bumpers and wheels), deep wall-to-wall carpets, padded leather upholstery, a full instrument panel, air-controlled right-hand window, a tape recorder with stereo units, air conditioning, sleeper heaters, a television, self-defrosting mirrors, tinted windshield, cab-controlled sliding fifth wheel, AM-FM radio, hot and cold running water and plug-in arrangements to heat coffee.

Cf. truck-stop commando, vanliner.

rolling stock: the tractors and trailers that make up a truck fleet.

Cf. flagship.

roster: when the dispatch department has no immediate assignment for a driver, the driver's name is entered on the dispatch roster. When he calls in after making his delivery, a driver will ask for his position on the roster—how many drivers (if any) are ahead of him and will be given loads before him. Most company's rosters are organized on a "first-in, first-out" basis.

Cf. bid run, brownie points, dispatch, roving team, relay, slip-seat operation.

roving team: a two-man operation which has no regular, specified run (such as a bid run) but is dispatched to a variety of destinations by the company.

Cf. concentrator, divorced, lead driver, married, navigator, shotgun.

r.p.m.: the revolutions per minute of the engine's crankshaft, generally expressed in hundreds as registered on the tractor's tachometer. The operating range for most diesel tractors is from about 1500 r.p.m. to 2200 r.p.m.

Cf. crankshaft, drive shaft, rev, tack, tattletale.

rubber: truck tires.

Syn.: baloneys, skins, irons.

Cf. cheater slicks, rider, singing, waffles.

rubber band drive: a tag axle powered by a rubber belt that is run off the tractor's drive axle.

Syn.: belt drive.

Cf. powered by rubber bands.

rub rails: the steel framework on the sides of a flat bed or single-drop trailer to which the chains holding down the load are fastened.

Cf. button her down, boomer, chains and binders, convertible.

run: to drive a route to a destination.

Cf. pull, turn.

run double: to run with a second driver, usually on a long-haul or cross-country trip. The truck can be kept running almost constantly because while one driver rests the other drives.

Cf. lead driver, roving team, shotgun, switch seats, two-man operation.

run legal: to transport commodities by truck in a way that meets all federal, state and local regulations.

Cf. believer, moonlighter, runnin' hot.

runnin' hot: **1.** running a rig illegally (overweight, out of log book time or without permits or authority).

Cf. believer, boondockin', Moonlight Express.

2. running a little behind schedule with a load that must be delivered by a specified time.

Cf. clock load, flyer, hot load.

running lights: a tractor-trailer's clearance lights.
Syn.: marker lights.
Cf. bus markers, driving lights, identification lights, rolling lighthouse, torpedoes.

running start: an advantage a trucker tries to gain by parking a few feet ahead of another trucker he's been running with; in this way (he thinks) he can get back out on the road faster.
Cf. beach, peel out.

Runs Empty Only: truckers' longhand for a Reo tractor.
Cf: **F**ix **o**r **R**epair **D**aily, **G**eneral **M**ess of **C**rap, **I**n **H**ock **C**onstantly.

run wide open: to drive a truck at full speed.
Syn.: build a fire, flying low, foot in the floorboards, haul the mail, pour on the coals.
Cf. tacked out.

S

saddle: the driver's seat.
Cf. eatin' concrete, make some miles, truck.

saddle mount: the practice of mounting the front axle of a tractor that is to be transported on the frame of the work tractor, leaving the rear axle of the carried tractor on the ground. In this way, two tractors can be relocated using only one driver.
Cf. double mount, full mount, triple mount.

saddle tanks: barrel-type fuel tanks that hold from

120 to 200 gallons. They hang from the side of the frame at the rear of the cab.

Cf. fuel gauge, full saddles, step tanks.

sagamore: a sagging trailer.

Cf. crate, sled.

sanders: one of the best winter aids to truckers, these are boxes located in front of each drive wheel that are manually operated from the inside of the cab to spray sand or chicken grit (coarse, groundup stones) onto the road to help the truck to maintain traction on icy hills.

Cf. irons, put on the iron, spin out.

sand hacker: a dump truck driver who hauls sand and gravel.

Cf. tipper.

scow: **1.** a low-sided trailer used for hauling pipe, steel, stone, gravel, scrap and similar cargo. **2.** any large trailer or tractor-trailer.

Cf. trailer types.

scratch one in: to grind gears in shifting.

Cf. cog stripper, gear jammer, split the cogs.

screamin' Jimmy: a G.M.C. engine; so named because of the high-pitched noise it makes when running.

Syn.: Detroit diesel, **G**arage **M**an's **C**ompanion, Hillbilly Special, Jimmy, screamin' Lena.

screamin' Lena: a G.M.C. engine.

Syn.: Detroit diesel, Hillbilly Special, screamin' Jimmy.

Cf. poor man's tractor, turnpike tightwad.

screw: a tractor with two drive axles.

Syn.: both axles pulling, full screw, twin screw, two axles pulling.

Cf. dead axle, live axle, spider, tag axle.

searcher: a Fuller Roadranger transmission; this name is applied west of the Mississippi because, if the transmission ever needs replacements there, you will be "searching" for parts.

Cf. deep-reduction valve, Roadranger, splitter.

Sears-Roebuck license: the license said to be held by an inferior driver.

Cf. aviator, boll weevil, cowboy, real amateur, sheep herder, tailboard artist.

second driver: the alternate driver in a two-man operation.

Syn.: copilot, shotgun, swamper.

Cf. concentrator, divorced, lead driver, married, navigator, ride shotgun, run double.

semi: **1.** a semi-trailer, or a trailer with only rear axles, as opposed to a full trailer, which has both front and rear axles. The front of the semi-trailer rests on the tractor or is supported by its landing gear.

Syn.: box, body.

Cf. landing gear, trailer.

2. the entire tractor-trailer unit.

Cf. truck.

Note: "Semi" is pronounced "sem-eye."

semi and pup: a double-bottom rig composed of a tractor, a semi-trailer, a converter dolly and a second, and much shorter, semi, or pup.

Syn.: deck and four-wheeler.

Cf. centipede, dual shorts, kite, kite without a tail, Michigan rig, pup, short bottom.

semi driver: a trucker.

Syn.: commercial tourist, double-clutchin' man, gear jammer, spinner.

Cf. line driver, over-the-road driver, truckologist, turnaround driver.

semi-floating axle: an axle assembly in which the weight of the vehicle and cargo rests on the axle instead of on the axle housing.

Cf. full-floating axle.

semi-trailer: a trailer that has only rear axles, as opposed to a trailer that has axles both in the front and in the rear. The front of a semi-trailer either rests on the tractor or is supported by its landing gear when independent of a tractor.

Syn.: body, semi.

Cf. full trailer, semi, truck, trailer types, truck-trailer.

set her down: to make a quick stop.

Syn.: spike it.

Cf. brakin' 'er down, dynamite the brakes, fannin' the brakes, reach for the air, shadow the brake.

set it up: **1.** to turn the governor up in order to increase engine r.p.m. **2.** to increase the fuel portion in the fuel-to-air ratio.

Syn.: open 'er up, turn the wick up.

Cf. cut 'er down, weaned out.

set of joints: a double-bottom rig; so named because there are three pivot points: the two fifth wheels and the tongue.

Syn.: doubles, twin trailers.

Cf. dual shorts, Michigan rig, train, triples.

set of racks: removable sides for a flat bed trailer.

Cf. open top, convertible.

set up: **1.** said of the brakes of either the tractor

or the trailer when they automatically go into effect and halt the vehicle, usually in the event of an air pressure loss.

Cf. breakaway valve, four-way relay emergency valve, hanging up.

2. refers to the specifications on a tractor, as in "How's your rig set up?"

Cf. specs.

shadow the brake: to touch the foot brake lightly when approaching a green or yellow light in order to be able to stop the rig easily and smoothly should the light change to red.

Cf. brakin' 'er down, clamp on the binders, fannin' the brakes, reach for the air, spike it, throw out the anchor.

shag: a small, city trailer.

Cf: city flyer.

shagging: spotting or parking trailers brought into a terminal by over-the-road drivers.

Cf. boss her, spotter, spot the body, yard bird, yard mule.

shake down the ashes: **1.** to crank the starter in an old-time truck.

Cf. armstrong starter, stew winder.

2. to start a truck.

Syn.: build a fire, fire it up, kick 'er over, wind 'er up.

shake the lights: **1.** to blink the tractor's headlights as a warning to other truckers. **2.** to flash the trailer's lights as a warning to truckers approaching from the rear.

Cf. give him the lights, give him the wind.

shanty hauler: a trucker who moves house trailers. His is an especially nerve-racking job because of crosswinds, narrow roads, low bridges, tight corners and the usually small, under-powered tractors used (in order to stay within the overall length limit). One of the most expensive and time-consuming headaches of these truckers is trying to satisfy the different interstate length limitations and placarding requirements ("wide load," "overwidth load" and others).

Syn.: shanty shaker, shanty shifter, trailer jock.

Cf. coach, trailer toter.

shanty shaker: a trucker who transports mobile homes.

Syn.: shanty hauler, shanty shifter.

Cf. stairstep, trailer hauler.

shanty shifter: a trucker who hauls mobile homes.

Syn.: shanty hauler, trailer jock.

Cf. coach, stairstep, trailer toter.

sheep herder: a driver of dubious ability. The term probably originated among bull haulers and reflected the enmity between cattlemen and sheep raisers.

Cf. boll weevil, cowboy, eight-miler, real amateur, tailboard artist.

shoat and goat conductor: a livestock hauler.

Syn.: grunt-and-squeal jockey.

Cf. bull hauler, bull rack, Pork Chop Express, possum belly, shoat boat.

shoat boat: a livestock trailer.

Syn.: bull rack, possum belly, pullman.

Cf. cackle crate, hog hauler, Pork Chop Express, shoat and goat conductor.

shortage: the difference between the amount of freight actually shipped and the amount marked on the bill of lading.
Cf. claim, overage.

short bottom: a combination with a converter dolly hooked to the rear of a semi; used to couple a second semi-trailer to the first.
Syn.: kite without a tail.
Cf. double-bottom rig, long double, triples, twin trailers.

short couple: a shortened reach on a logging combination that reduces the overall length of the tractor-trailer by pulling the reach up closer to the cab.
Cf. pole trailer, reach, stinger.

short logger: long bunks mounted on the front and rear of a pole trailer to carry the log load.
Cf. muley cow, pole trailer, reach, stick hauler, stinger.

short-nose: describes a conventional cab with a short hood.
Cf. bonnet, long-nose.

shotgun: an alternate driver in a truck.
Syn.: copilot, second driver, swamper.
Cf. divorced, lead driver, married, ride shotgun, run double, two-man operation.

shovel: to load freight in a hasty and sloppy manner.
Cf.: claim, fingerprint, hand job.

shroud: a protective covering or splash shield made of rubber or metal and placed anywhere on a truck—under the hood, above the steer-

ing axle—to eliminate mud splashes from the tires.
Cf. mud flaps.

shut 'er down: to turn off the ignition.
Cf. kick 'er over.

shut out: to miss making a delivery or pickup at a company because their loading or unloading time has just come to an end.
Cf. lay over.

shutters: louvers that are located between the tractor's grill and the radiator of the engine and that open and close like venetian blinds. They have a thermostatic control triggered by heat from the engine to maintain a constant operating temperature. They open when the heat is too high and close when it is too low.
Cf. bandaged up, winter front.

sick horse: a tractor with little power.
Syn.: dog, gutless wonder.
Cf. horse, oakie blower, supercharger.

side boards: boards used to extend the sides of a dump body in order to increase the load capacity.
Syn.: cheater boards, hungry boards.
Cf. dump body, tipper, water-level hauling capacity.

side car: the U-model Mack conventional cab, which was specifically designed to counteract the difficulty drivers experienced in readjusting their perspective when they switched from a cabover to a conventional tractor. The cab is not centered but set to the left side of the tractor, enabling the driver to see the road clearly to the left and to the left rear.

Syn.: sidewinder.
Cf. Mack.

side dump: a trailer body that is emptied from the side.
Cf. bottom dumps, hopper body, tipper.

sidewinder: nickname for the U-model Mack tractor, a conventional cab with the driver's compartment set off center, to the left.
Syn.: side car.
Cf. anteater, B-model, cherry picker, Mack.

singer: **1.** a chain-drive truck, now a memory of trucking's early days.
Cf. chain-drive wallet, slave ship, sucker brake.
2. a new or recapped tire that has an unbroken tread line and creates a lot of road noise.
Syn.: cop caller, Pennsylvania caps.
Cf. singing, surface cap.

singing: a sound truck tires make when a rig is driven at high speed.
Cf. cop caller, duals, rubber.

single axle: **1.** a tractor with one front axle and one rear axle.
Cf. four-by-two.
2. a semi-trailer with only one axle instead of the more common tandem axles.
Syn.: skinny axle.
Cf. sliding tandem, spread, tandem, triaxle.

single-drop trailer: a flat bed trailer with a drop in the top surface of the frame. For instance, in a forty-foot single-drop trailer, the higher level (at the front end) is twelve feet long, there is a one-foot drop, and the lower level is twenty-eight feet long.

Syn.: drop-deck flat, step-deck trailer, step flat.

Cf. leveling block.

single mount: a saddle-mount operation involving one towing vehicle and one towed vehicle.

Cf. double mount, full mount, saddle mount, triple mount.

single operation: a way of operating a truck that involves only one driver, as opposed to a two-man operation in which two men drive the rig.

Cf. concentrator, navigator.

single reduction: a rear end assembly with one pinion gear and one ring gear, the purposes of which are to reduce engine speed and to transmit power from the drive shaft to the wheels.

Cf. banjo, double reduction, pig, rear end assembly.

six-banger: a six-cylinder diesel engine.

Cf. bucket, bumble bee, four-banger.

six-by-six: a twin screw tractor in which the steering axle is also a drive axle (Army usage).

Cf. four-by-two, F.W.D., six-by-two.

six-by-two: a tandem-axle tractor (Army usage).

Cf. four-by-two, six-by-six.

six-wheeler: a tandem-axle tractor; in this usage, the steering axle wheels count as two and each of the four duals counts as one.

Syn.: ten-wheeler.

Cf. four-by-two, six-by-six, six-by-two.

skinnie axle: a single axle on a trailer.

Syn.: single axle.

Cf. tandem, triaxle.

skins: tires.

Syn.: baloneys, rubber.

Cf. cheater slicks, duals, dusting, irons, kick the doughnuts, pumpkin, waffles.

skip gears: to drive a tractor by using only every second or third gear of the transmission; it is possible only when the tractor-trailer is partly loaded, when it is deadheading, or when the trucker is driving the tractor bobtail.

Cf. gearboxes, split the cogs.

slack adjuster: a device located on the trailer tandems that is used to tighten or to loosen the brake shoe.

Cf. four-way relay emergency valve, hanging up.

slave ship: a solid-tired truck. Solid rubber tires were used on trucks before the invention of tires with inner tubes.

sled: **1.** an old, worn-out trailer.

Syn.: club.

Cf. crate, sagamore.

2. a trailer that pulls hard because of design or wind resistance.

Cf. drag.

sledgehammer mechanic: a mechanic who beats parts off with a hammer or some other tool instead of removing them with a wrench.

Cf. chief hood lifter, grease monkey, ice man, maniac.

sleeper: **1.** the bunk compartment behind the driver's seat in any tractor.

Syn.: slumber slot.

Cf. pajama wagon, suicide box.

2. the tractor which has a sleeper may also be referred to as a sleeper.

Cf. day cab, pull a sleep job, straight.

sleeper box: a sleeping compartment mounted on a truck frame to the rear of the cab; not an integral part of the cab.
Syn.: coffin box, suicide box.
Cf. pajama wagon, sweat box.

sleeper cab: a tractor in which an adjoining bunk area is located behind the driver's seat.
Cf. coffin box, pajama wagon, slumber slot.

sleeperette: an Emeryville-style tractor that is not intended for sleeper operation because it has rear and side windows.
Cf. look-see window, picture windows.

sleeve job: a partial engine overhaul in which sleeves, pistons, rings and bearings are changed.

slider: a sliding fifth wheel.
Cf. air slider, cup and saucer.

sliding fifth wheel: a fifth wheel whose location on the tractor's frame can be adjusted to suit trailers of different lengths and cargoes of different weights. This is made possible by sliding the coupling device backward or forward between the heavy parallel beams set on the frame. For instance, moving the fifth wheel forward places more weight on the tractor's steering axle and shortens the overall length of the combination.
Syn.: air slider, slider.
Cf. fifth wheel, kingpin, pin setting.

sliding tandem: a tandem-axle unit beneath the trailer that can be moved forward or backward to suit the requirements of the weight of the cargo and to distribute the weight better. To adjust a sliding tandem, the trucker applies the trailer brakes, releases the pins holding the tandem unit in position, then moves the tractor-trailer forward or backward over the axle unit.

Cf. fishtail, stretched out, West Coast tandem.

slip-seat operation: a process involving two tractors and one driver in which the driver arrives at a terminal with one rig, leaves it, and continues on with another truck. This is in contrast to a relay, which involves one truck and a number of drivers.

Cf. relay.

slop bucket: a water can used to fill the radiator of a tractor.

Cf. slop the hogs.

slop the hogs: to fill the radiator of a truck with water.

Cf. punctured lung, slop bucket, water dog.

slumber slot: the bunk compartment behind the driver's seat in a tractor.

Syn.: sleeper.

Cf. coffin box, pajama wagon, sleeper box, sweat box.

smitty: a glass-packed muffler.

Cf. bark, buckhorn pipes, gutted, spittoon muffler, twin chimneys.

smoke him: to pass another vehicle.

Cf. give him the lights.

smoker: **1.** any diesel tractor; so named because the older diesels emitted excessive smoke from the exhaust.

Cf. diesel, gas job.

2. a load of cigarettes.
Cf. crate of sand, load of suds, red label load, zephyr haul.
3. a tractor that gives off excessive exhaust smoke.
Cf. Indian talk, lay a trail.

smokestack: the exhaust unit alongside a tractor.
Cf. bark, goathorns, gutted, smitty, spittoon muffler, talk, twin chimneys, woodpecker.

smokin' in high gear: driving a truck at full speed; really moving out down the road.
Syn.: big hole it, build a fire, turn it on, tacked out.
Cf. gettin' stretched, throwin' flame.

smooth-side: describes a box trailer with smooth sides.
Cf. corrugated, rib-side.

snub-nose: a cabover tractor; so nicknamed because of its straight profile.
Syn.: blunt-nose, flat face, pug.
Cf. alligator, flip top.

sock it to her: to drive fast.
Syn.: flying low, open 'er up, pour on the coals, tacked out.
Cf. aviator, highballer, lead foot.

soft pedal: to use a gentle braking action.
Cf. hard pedal, shadow the brake, spike it.

solo: 1. to drive a tractor without a trailer.
Syn.: bareback, bobtail, loose horse.
Cf. drop the box.
2. to drive a rig alone when the driver in question is usually part of a two-man operation.

Cf. divorced, single operation.

spaceship: the International Harvester tilt-cab model 190; it has proportionately large windows and looks like a cruising spaceship.

Cf. bifocal International, corn binder, two-story Emeryville, West Coast binder.

specialized carrier: a carrier who hauls specifically named commodities, generally into wide areas, as contrasted with a company that handles general freight. Examples are the heavy hauler, bean hauler, household goods hauler, bull hauler, oil field hauler and shanty hauler.

Cf. common carrier, contract carrier, for-hire carrier, private carrier, weeder geese hauler.

specs: truck or tractor specifications.

Cf. set up.

Spicer: a make of transmission that uses one gearbox and one gearshift lever. A driver puts the gearshift into the first gear; to get into the next higher gear, he flips a lever on the gearshift and returns it to the same hole. The remaining shift positions are handled in the same way. When the trucker has run through the first round of gears, he raises another button on the gearshift, brings the gearshift back to the first hole, and repeats the procedure to obtain successively higher gears. In addition to the type of Spicer transmission described above, Spicer makes all types of main and auxiliary gearboxes. They are regarded as superior transmission manufacturers because of the long life and service of their products.

Cf. gearboxes, four-by-four, mix-master special, Roadranger.

spider: a tandem-axle tractor in which the first axle of the tandem unit is both a half axle (single tires instead of duals) and a dead axle. The rearmost axle is the drive axle. The purpose of a spider is to enable the rig to scale more cargo weight. These rigs are called spiders because the steering axle and the half axle turn together; that and the short wheelbase make the tractor look like a spider.

Cf. bogies, live axle, peg leg, pusher, steering axle, trail axle, twin screw.

spike it: to rapidly bring a rig to a dead stop and to remain stopped.

Cf. beach, dynamite the brakes, set 'er down, throw out the anchor.

spinner: a truck driver.

Syn.: big rig man, commercial highway engineer, double-clutchin' man, gear shifter, line driver, semi driver.

Cf. trucker.

spin out: to lose traction on a slippery road.

Cf. buy up an orchard, put on the iron, sanders, total it out, waffles.

spittoon muffler: a little, short muffler on a smokestack.

Cf. build a fire, gutted, smitty, twin chimneys.

spit valve: a valve in the air line system of a tractor that emits some air each time the brakes are applied. It keeps condensed water and moisture from collecting in the air system and is important for the safe operation of a tractor.

Syn.: moisture-release valve.

Cf. air brakes, low-air warning device.

split-arc: to cut a corner.

Syn.: bite a turn, chop a turn.

Cf. need a hinge, wrap 'er around the bend.

split gears: to shift the auxiliary gearshift to obtain the different gear ratios available for each gear in the main box. For instance, in a triplex transmission, manipulation of the auxiliary gearshift while leaving the main gearshift in, say, fourth gear will split fourth gear three times.

Cf. four-way split, split the cogs, three-way split, two-way split.

split-shaft PTO: usually seen employed in a rig with a mixer or a cable winch; the split-shaft **p**ower **t**ake **o**ff gearbox is mounted in the gear train in somewhat the same way as an auxiliary transmission. It can transfer full power to the mixer or winch.

Cf. front PTO.

split-shifting: simultaneously shifting gears in both the main and the auxiliary gearboxes.

Cf. mix-master special.

split-shiftin' gloves: gloves worn by a trucker while driving; by tradition, these gloves are almost invariably white.

Syn.: two-speed gloves.

Cf. chain-drive wallet, double-clutchin' boots, gearshift cap.

splitter: **1.** the mechanism that operates part of the thirteen-speed Roadranger transmission. It divides fifth, sixth, seventh and eighth gears into a direct and an overdrive gear for each.

Cf. deep-reduction valve, Roadranger, searcher.

2. the activating knob, lever or button on a Roadranger or on a Spicer transmission.

Cf. Spicer.

split the cogs: to change gears (Australian usage).

Syn.: kick 'em.

Cf. drag down, feather, grab one, float the gears, knock it down, skip gears.

spooks: rough narrow bars made of a tar and stone mixture that are built across a highway in the road surface just before a toll booth or stop sign and whose purpose is to warn oncoming vehicles to slow down and to wake up sleepy drivers.

Cf. berm, holy road.

spot mirror: a small, round convex mirror used to provide a trucker with visibility to the rear of his vehicle.

Syn.: peek-a-boo mirrors, powderpuff.

Cf. blind side, West Coast mirrors.

spotter: **1.** a terminal worker who parks trucks or relocates trailers brought in by over-the-road drivers.

Syn. yard bird.

Cf. shagging, spot the box, yard mule.

2. a supervisor who checks the activities of drivers while they are on the road.

Syn. checker.

Cf. chaser.

spot the body: to pick up, to park or to unhook from a semi-trailer in a terminal or truck yard.

Syn.: spot the box.

Cf. drop the box, shagging, spotter.

spot the box: to pick up, to park or to unhook from a semi-trailer of the van variety in a terminal or truck yard.

Syn.: spot the body.

Cf. break the unit, swamper, unlatch, yard mule.

spread: a trailer with a separation greater than four feet between the two rear axles of a tandem trailer or between the first and second or the second and third axles of a triaxle trailer. A spread trailer is legally allowed to carry a heavier cargo than a tandem because the weight is not concentrated over one area.

Cf. Michigan spread, Ohio spread, tandem spread, three-legged trailer, three nines, triaxle, widespread.

sprinkle a load: to make quick stop offs to partially unload a trailer.

Syn.: string it.

Cf. peddle run.

square wheels: Dayton or spoke wheels on a truck.

Syn.: manure-spreader wheels, wobblers.

Cf. babymoon hubcaps, Budd wheels.

Note: Most West Coast rigs have Budd wheels; although they cost more, Budds are stronger and make the tires run more true.

squealer: a recording device in a tractor that automatically notes the number of miles and hours driven, the speed, number and frequency of stops and other pertinent daily statistics.

Syn.: tachograph, tattletale.

Cf. hub-o-meter, milograph, tachometer, tack.

stack: a vertical exhaust pipe on a diesel rig.

Cf. dual stacks, smokestack, twin chimneys.

stairstep: a process by which a shanty hauler moves two house trailers to the same destination. He starts out from one point with the first trailer, drops it at a second point, and returns to the first point for the second trailer. He transports the second trailer to the second point, picks up the first trailer, hauls it to a third point, returns to the second point for the second trailer—and continues the process until the haul is completed.

Cf. shanty shifter.

stay on his tail: to follow another truck closely, especially when only the driver of the lead truck knows the route.

Cf. rat race.

steamboat: a diesel truck.

Syn.: diesel, horse, oil burner, rig, scow, semi, smoker, widow-maker.

steel jockey: a trucker who hauls steel.

Syn.: iron hauler.

Cf. painted scrap-iron hauler, Pig Iron Express, suicide coil.

steely: a brake used in the western United States that is made of a magnesium-steel alloy brake shoe in a steel drum; favored in hilly or mountainous terrain because the hotter a steely becomes the greater is its holding power.

Syn.: hot foot, hot shoe, mag brake.

Cf. air brakes, Emma Jesse brake, Jake brake, Johnson bar, slack adjuster, sucker brake.

steering axle: **1.** the foremost axle of the tractor, in contrast to the drive axle(s) to the rear. This axle determines the direction the combination will take as determined by the driver; the drive axles determine the rate of progression. **2.** sometimes a tandem-spread trailer (of the type in which the tandem unit is located in front of the trailer's single axle) has the single (rearmost) axle controlled in much the same manner as a tractor's steering axle. This facilitates the driver's control of the trailer's movement.

Cf. dead axle, drivers, pusher, spider, tandem spread, three-legged trailer.

stem winder: **1.** a hand-cranked starter on an old-fashioned truck.

Syn.: armstrong starter, stew winder.

2. a truck that has a hand-cranked starter.

Cf. give her the works, shake down the ashes.

step bumper: a bumper with a small platform that is used as a step to the cargo-carrying body; usually seen on city straight jobs.

step-deck trailer: a flat bed trailer with a drop in the top surface of the frame. In a typical forty-foot step-deck trailer, the front end is twelve feet long, there is a one-foot drop, and the lower level is twenty-eight feet long.

Syn.: drop-deck flat, step flat, step trailer, single-drop trailer.

Cf. double-drop trailer, leveling block.

step flat: a flat bed or flat bottom trailer with a drop in the top surface of the frame. In a typical step flat, the higher level, which is at the trailer's front end, is twelve feet long, the drop is one foot in depth, and the lower level is twenty-eight feet long. The overall length of the trailer is still forty feet.

Syn.: drop-deck flat, single-drop trailer, step-deck trailer.

Cf. leveling block.

step tanks: fuel tanks on a tractor that are located below the doors and have an indentation that serves as a step to permit access to the cab.

Cf. full saddles, saddle tanks.

step trailer: a flat bed trailer with a drop in the top surface of the frame. In the usual forty-foot step trailer, the front end is twelve feet long, there is a one-foot drop, and the lower level is twenty-eight feet long.

Syn.: drop-deck flat, single-drop trailer, step-deck trailer, step flat.

stew winder: **1.** a hand-cranked starter in a truck.

Syn.: armstrong starter, stem winder.

2. a truck that has a hand-cranked starter.

Cf. shake down the ashes.

stick hauler: a trucker who transports logs.

Cf. pole trailer, pony wheels, short couple, short logger.

stick-um or goo: **1.** tape used to affix trip lease signs to the tractor's doors.

Cf. cardboard driver.

2. the same tape is also used to cover the exhaust stacks on farm tractors or Caterpillar machines in transit.

stinger: **1.** the hook on a cable at the rear of a

truck (logging usage). **2.** the hook at the back of a tractor to which the reach connects.

Cf. lunette, pintle hook, reach, stick hauler.

stirrups: **1.** punched out or recessed holes in a tractor's bumper that provide toeholds so that a trucker or station attendant can reach the tractor's windshield to clean it. **2.** angle irons mounted under the bumper to make it easy to clean the windshield.

stove and fiddle: a heater and a radio in a cab.

Cf. hillbilly operahouse, Hunter heater, noisemaker.

straight: **1.** a tractor, either conventional or cab-over, that does not have a sleeper.

Syn.: day cab.

Cf. pajama wagon, sleeper box.

2. a livestock trailer with a straight frame rather than a drop frame.

Cf. possum belly.

straight job: a small truck whose body is built directly onto the chassis; commonly used in industrial areas.

Cf. city flyer, combinations.

stretched out: describes a trailer on which the tandems are slid all the way to the rear.

Cf. fishtail, sliding tandem, West Coast tandem.

stretch flat: a flat bed trailer that has a telescoping body so that the length of the trailer may be increased or decreased for cargoes of varying lengths.

Syn.: stretch trailer, table top.

Cf. expandable lowboy, pole trailer.

stretch lowboy: a lowboy trailer whose length can be increased to suit the requirements of different cargoes.

Cf. expandable lowboy.

stretch out: to lengthen the interaxle bridge by moving the fifth wheel all the way back and sliding the trailer tandems all the way to the rear; an advantageous maneuver when passing through states in which bridge laws are enforced.

Cf. bridge formula, sliding fifth wheel, sliding tandem, West Coast rig.

stretch trailer: a flat bed trailer that has a telescoping body that can be increased or decreased in length to accommodate cargoes of varying lengths.

Syn.: stretch flat, table top.

Cf. pole trailer, stretch lowboy.

string it: to partially unload a trailer by making a series of stop offs, delivering the cargo along the way; especially said of unloading pipe throughout a new housing development.

Syn.: sprinkle a load.

strip her: to disassemble a tractor; especially, to salvage parts from a junked tractor.

Cf. kit, residenter.

struck capacity: the load capacity of a dump trailer when the load is exactly level with the sides and is not heaped up in the center; this is equivalent to the water level.

Cf. cheater boards, water-level hauling capacity.

stump jumper: a large steel plate mounted beneath

the engine to keep foreign objects from damaging it; usually found on tractors used for logging.
Syn.: engine guard.

sucker brake: the old-time vacuum brake, the ancestor of today's air brake.
Cf. air brakes, East Coast hookup, hot shoe, Jake brake, West Coast hookup.

suicide box: a box sleeper added on to a conventional cab; so named because in a jackknife accident the most hazardous place to be is in the sleeper.
Syn.: coffin box.
Cf. day cab, drom box, pajama wagon, slumber slot.

suicide coil: a steel coil loaded onto the trailer with the eye of the coil crosswise on the trailer instead of loaded with the eye running longitudinally; so named because, if the chains holding the coil in position were to break, there would be nothing to keep the coil from rolling forward into the tractor in an emergency stop.
Cf. boomer, chains and binders, iron hauler, steel jockey.

suicide jockey: a trucker who hauls nitroglycerin —his rig is known as a boom wagon, of course.
Cf. dangerous articles, red label load.

summertime truck: a truck that is hard to start in the winter.
Cf. ether lock, mothballs.

sunshine driver: a trucker who will drive in good weather only.
Syn.: fair-weather driver.

Cf. windshield wiper-itis.

sunshine tarps: tarps that have numerous holes and tears in them; they "let the sunshine in."
Syn.: religious tarps.
Cf. button her up, tarps.

supercharger: a type of blower; a unit with curved revolving pieces driven by mechanic power from the engine whose purpose is to force air into the intake manifold at higher than atmospheric pressure. A supercharger increases engine power and performance. Another type of blower is the turbocharger; the difference between the two is that the supercharger is gear-driven and the turbocharger is run by exhaust gases.
Cf. blower, oakie blower.

surface cap: a recap on the surface of a tire that bears on the road, as opposed to a full cap.
Syn.: cap.
Cf. full cap, singers.

swamper: **1.** a man who handles freight, loading and unloading trucks at a dock.
Syn.: dock walloper.
Cf. chaser.
2. a helper or alternate driver riding in a truck.
Syn.: copilot, second driver, shotgun.
Cf. lead driver.

sweat box: a sleeper cab, especially if it has a poor ventilation system.
Cf. coffin box, pajama wagon, slumber slot, sweat shop.

sweat puller: a hard-driving truck.
Cf. kidney buster.

sweat shop: a cab with poor ventilation.
Cf. sweat box.

swede: a metal pipe used to gain leverage when tightening the chains and binders on a load.
Syn.: cheater bar.
Cf. boom it down, button her up.

swindle sheet: the daily log book, mandatory for all drivers.
Syn.: lie sheet.
Cf. log book.

swing brackets: the folding brackets that extend if needed from the sides of a lowboy trailer; should the cargo be wider than the trailer, planks are run across the tops of the outstretched brackets to receive the additional width.
Syn.: outriggers.
Cf. beam trailer, double-drop lowboy, expandable lowboy, gooseneck lowboy, level-deck lowboy.

swinger: a big load.
Cf. clock load, flyer, hot load, load of postholes, zephyr haul.

swingin' beef: the sides of slaughtered beef that are suspended from special racks in a trailer.
Cf. meat hauler, railer.

switcher: **1.** a man who moves trailers in a terminal.
Syn.: spotter, yard man.
Cf. shagging.
2. a company driver who drives a different tractor-trailer on every run.
Cf. hobo.
3. a driver who switches trailers at a terminal

or at an exchange point; that is, he exchanges an empty trailer for a loaded one.

Cf. relay, slip-seat operation.

switch seats: to swap off driving duties in a two-man operation. This enables the drivers to keep the truck running almost constantly, except for fuel and meal stops.

Cf. lead driver, run double, slip-seat operation.

T

table top: a flat bed trailer that has a telescoping body so that the length can be increased or decreased to accommodate varying cargoes.

Syn.: stretch flat, stretch trailer.

tachograph: a recording device in a tractor that automatically notes the number of miles driven, the speed, the number of stops and other pertinent statistics.

Syn.: squealer, tattletale.

Cf. milograph, tack.

tachometer: a device in the tractor, located on the instrument panel, that indicates the revolutions per minute of the crankshaft.

Syn.: tack.

Cf. grab one, knock it down, lugging, milograph, overspeed, tacked out, windmill.

tack: short for tachometer or tachograph.

Cf. hub-o-meter, milograph, odometer.

tacked out: **1.** to have a truck tacked out means that the driver has steadily progressed through all the tractor's gears and is running the rig at full speed.

Syn.: all stretched out, open 'er up, run wide open, top off, turn it on.

Cf. back off, build a fire, floorboard it, hook 'er into high, pulling gear, smoke him.

2. to run an engine at top r.p.m. in any gear.

Cf. governor, windmill.

tag axle: the hindmost axle of a tandem-axle tractor if that axle serves only to support additional gross weight, allowing the trucker to haul a greater payload. A tag axle does not transmit power to the wheels, as does a drive axle.

Syn.: dead axle, trail axle.

Cf. belt drive, bogies, live axle, pusher, spider, twin screw.

tailboard artist: a driver who believes his driving to be flawless.

Syn.: truck jockey.

Cf. boll weevil, sheep herder, truckologist, truck-stop commando.

tailgate it: to carry freight from the nose to the back of a trailer.

Cf. chimney sweep run, hand job, shovel.

tailgating: following another truck or car too closely, which invites an accident if the leading vehicle must slow up or stop suddenly.

Cf. jackknife, pile up, rat race, stay on his tail, total it out.

talk: a tractor is said to talk when its smokestack(s) produce a loud, clear sound.

Cf. bark, build a fire, tacked out.

tandem: **1.** two pairs of duals mounted together on

a trailer.

Cf. duals, floats.

2. a semi-trailer with two rear axles. Tandem axles must have a fifty-inch separation between axles; tandems may be either fixed at one position or adjustable in location under the bed.

Cf. skinnie axle, sliding tandem, tandem spread, West Coast tandem.

3. a tractor with one front axle and two rear axles: a tandem-axle tractor.

Syn.: six-wheeler, ten-wheeler.

4. generally speaking, a tractor-trailer.

Cf. tractor-trailer, truck.

tandem drive: tandem axles on a tractor, both of which serve to propel the vehicle.

Syn.: drivers, full screw, twin screw.

Cf. live axle, pusher, tag axle, both axles pulling, two axles pulling.

tandem spread: a triaxle trailer of either of the following types: the first has a single axle (close to the center of the trailer) and a spread of nine feet followed by a tandem-axle unit; the second has the axle order reversed, with the tandem unit located near the center of the trailer, followed by a nine-foot spread and then the single axle.

Syn.: three-legged trailer.

Cf. air-lift axle, spread, steering axle, three nines, wide-spread.

tandem-tandem: a rig composed of a tandem-axle tractor and a tandem-axle trailer.

Syn.: eighteen-wheel rig, five-axle rig.

Cf. eight-wheeler.

tanker: a specially designed trailer used for the transportation of liquids and gases.
Cf. baffle, trailer types.

tap dancer: a delivery truck driver.
Cf. bundle buggy, straight job.

tariff: a schedule or system of rates for the determination of freight charges by the carrier. The tariffs must by law be posted with the Interstate Commerce Commission.
Cf. bill of lading, commodity, minnie, rate.

tarp: the tarpaulin(s) used to cover a load of cargo liable to weather damage on a flat bed, lowboy or open top trailer.
Cf. button her up, rag top, sunshine tarps.

tattletale: a sealed tachograph in a tractor that simultaneously records a truck's speed and the time of day, thus producing a record of driving hours and stops. Installed by large companies to check on driver efficiency and running time, tattletales are, needless to say, unpopular with drivers.
Syn.: squealer.
Cf. tack.

Teamster: a unionized truck driver; a member of the International Brotherhood of Teamsters. The term is used because when the union was started in 1888 it banded together dray horse or heavy cartage drivers, better known as teamsters. The name was retained even after the changeover to mechanized transport began in 1910, but truck drivers gradually replaced the original teamsters.
Cf. I.B.T.

ten-speed: a ten-speed Roadranger transmission.

Cf. Roadranger, searcher.

ten-wheeler: a tandem-axle tractor; so named because each wheel and tire is counted.
Syn.: six-wheeler.
Cf. eight-wheeler, eighteen-wheel rig.

Texas Autocar: tongue-in-cheek truckese for a Chevrolet tractor.
Syn.: Detroit vibrator, Texas KW.

Texas KW: **1.** generally speaking, any tractor that is not an authentic Kenworth. **2.** any truck-tractor manufactured by Chevrolet.
Syn.: Detroit vibrator, Texas Autocar.

T-five: short for Toledo 5, the name given to the group of truck stops adjacent to exit 5 on the Ohio Turnpike. Although the nearest town is Stony Ridge, Ohio, T-five is named for Toledo, Ohio, which is the largest city in the immediate vicinity.
Cf. coffee pot, fuel stop, heartburn palace, truck-o-tel, truck stop.

Thermo King: a brand of refrigeration unit mounted on insulated vans to keep the interior at a specific temperature for the preservation of a perishable cargo.
Cf. bunker, cold blow, ice man, reefer.

thirteenth gear: the neutral gear position in a twelve-speed transmission; so referred to when the trucker throws the transmission out of gear to permit the vehicle's momentum to carry it down hill.
Syn.: eleventh gear, Georgia overdrive, Jewish overdrive, Mexican overdrive, midnight overdrive.
Cf. wobbly hole.

three-legged trailer: a triaxle trailer that has a tandem unit located near the center of the trailer, followed by a nine-foot spread and a single axle, which is a steering axle that enables the driver to control its movement better.
Syn.: peg leg.
Cf. spread, tandem spread, three nines, widespread, West Coast spread.

three nines: a double spread on a trailer; a triaxle trailer with a nine-foot spread or separation between each axle.
Cf. spread, three-legged trailer.

three-speed axle: a drive axle that has low, intermediate and high ratios. In a tractor with a three-speed axle, there is one gearshift, which operates a four- or five-speed main box; the three speed gradients of the rear axle are gotten by manipulating a button on the gearshift lever.
Cf. main box, two-speed axle, unishift.

three-way split: a three-speed auxiliary transmission, the split being the low side, direct, and the high side.
Cf. duplex, four-way split, over and under, triplex, two-way split.

throttle shakes: a nervous reaction in a driver's right, or accelerator, leg that makes it difficult for him to maintain constant pressure on the accelerator; generally caused by a narrowly avoided accident on the road.
Cf. foot feed, foot in the floorboards.

throwin' flame: showing a flame or a red glow at the end of the smokestack(s) on a tractor. Such a tractor is not running most efficiently because the ratio of fuel to air in the engine is too high. When such wasted fuel is exhausted from the stack, it ignites; in the daytime it shows as diesel smoke, while at night the flame of the igniting fuel is visible.

Cf: Indian talk, lay a trail.

throw out the anchor: to apply the brakes.

Syn.: clamp on the binders, grab some air, set her down, spike it.

Cf. brake it off, dynamite the brakes.

thumb buster: **1.** a spinning steering wheel. **2.** a steering device used to enable the driver to spin the steering wheel fast in a cranking fashion (as in turning the truck); so named because when the wheel returns to its central position the knob can hit and injure an unaware driver.

tied up: refers to an obstructed highway.

Cf. line, religious states.

tightwad tractor: any tractor that has a low weight, low initial investment and a low upkeep; a favorite of steel haulers because it can keep down the gross vehicle weight and permit a heavier payload. A trucker with a tandem-axle tractor weighing only 10,000 pounds and an aluminum flat bed trailer of 7,000 pounds could haul a legal payload of 56,000 pounds.

Syn.: moneymaker.

Cf.: turnpike tightwad.

tilt cab: a cabover; so named because in order to get at the engine the driver's compartment of the tractor must be pivoted upward and forward almost ninety degrees.

Syn.: flip top.
Cf. alligator, two-story Emeryville.

tipper: a dump truck.
Cf. bottom dumps, hopper body, quick disconnect couplers, rear dump, sand hacker, wet line kit.

tire billy: a short club with a lead-filled head that truckers use to test the amount of air pressure in a rig's tires (by the sound a tire makes when it is struck). A tire billy saves a driver from kicking the tires and risking subsequent foot injury. Tire billies were originally designed for the protection of drivers in case of physical danger or assault.
Cf. kick the doughnuts, pumpkin.

tongue: the coupling device between the two trailers in a double-bottom combination.
Syn.: dollies, double hookup, jo-jo, whippletree.
Cf. dual shorts, kite, long double, rolling doughnuts, set of joints, train.

top off: to attain the top speed of which a tractor is capable.
Syn.: all stretched out, tacked out.
Cf. build a fire, haul the mail, pour on the coals.

torpedoes: large, bullet-shaped clearance lights on a tractor.
Syn.: bullet lights, bus markers.
Cf. clearance lights, dual spots, indentification lights, running lights.

total it out: to wreck a truck completely.
Cf. belly up, buy up an orchard, jackknife, pile up, spin out.

tow hooks: hooks, generally found on a tractor's bumper, by which it can be towed or pulled.
Cf. rock it.

tractor: the forepart, or power unit, of a tractor-trailer combination. Tractors are often named for the number of their rear axles: a single-axle tractor has two axles (one steering, one drive axle); a tandem-axle tractor has three axles (one steering and two drive axles, or one drive and one tag axle).
Syn.: diesel, horse, rig, unit, widow-maker.
Cf. cabover, combinations, conventional cab, dead axle, drive axle, pusher, spider, steering axle, tandem drive, trailer.

tractor-protection valve: a valve in the tractor that, if an air line breaks, automatically closes when the air pressure drops to between thirty and forty pounds. By closing off the air to the trailer, it conserves some of the air in the tractor.
Syn.: breakaway valve.
Cf. air pressure gauge, four-way relay emergency valve.

tractor-trailer: a long, two-component over-the-road truck made up of a power unit and a body in or on which the cargo rests.
Syn.: big rig, combination, rig, semi, tandem, widow-maker.
Cf. rolling stock, straight job, tractor, trailer, trucker, truck-trailer.

tractor types: a tractor can be a conventional or a cabover, a sleeper or a straight cab, and it can have a single axle or tandem axles. On the basis of appearance, therefore, tractors can be divided into eight categories.

Cf. cabover, conventional cab, day cab, single axle, sleeper cab, straight, tandem.

trail axle: the hindmost dead axle of a tandem-axle rig when that axle is a dead axle and not a drive axle.

Syn.: tag axle.

Cf. dead axle, joe dog, pusher, spider.

trailer: the second unit of a tractor-trailer combination, the part in or on which the cargo rests. Trailers can be of several kinds: semitrailer, or one with only rear wheels; full trailer, which has wheels both front and rear; single-axle; tandem-axle, either sliding or fixed; triaxle; spread; tandem spread; three nines.

Syn.: body, box, scow, semi, tandem.

Cf. trailer types.

trailer connections: the hoses and cable that extend from the tractor to the trailer and furnish it with air for the brakes and electricity for the tail and clearance lights.

Syn.: trolley lines.

Cf. air hose, glad hand, pigtail.

trailer hauler: a small truck-tractor set up to pull a forty-foot trailer; especially, a trailer designed to carry two, three or four camper trailers.

Cf. shanty shaker, trailer toter.

trailer jock: a trucker who hauls house trailers.

Syn.: shanty shifter, shanty shaker.

Cf. coach, stairstep, trailer hauler, trailer toter.

trailer toter: a truck set up to pull house trailers. Some have an expandable frame that permits an overall length of seventy-five feet.
Cf. coach, shanty shifter, stairstep, trailer hauler, trailer jock.

trailer types: trailers can be classified under two general categories: those that enclose their cargo and those on which cargo is in the open and tied down:

(A) enclosed cargo trailers:
- (1) van or box trailer
  - (a) freight box
  - (b) reefer—insulated body
  - (c) drop bottom
- (2) open top
  - (a) rag top
  - (b) converto-van
  - (c) dump truck
    - (1) rear dump—tipper
    - (2) bottom dump—hopper body
    - (3) side dump
- (3) tanker
- (4) cement body
- (5) livestock pullman
  - (a) straight—bull rack
  - (b) possum belly

(B) trailers on which cargo is in the open and tied down:
- (1) flat bed or platform
  - (a) stretch flat
  - (b) single-drop (step-deck flat)
  - (c) convertible
- (2) lowboy
  - (a) level-deck

(b) double-drop (double-deck lowboy)
(c) expandable lowboy
(d) stretch lowboy
(e) detachable gooseneck
(3) pole trailer
(4) car transporter

train: a double-bottom rig that has forty-foot trailers.
Syn.: doubles, long double, set of joints, twin trailers.
Cf. dual shorts, Michigan rig, rolling doughnuts, semi and pup, trainman's license, triples.

trainman's license: a special license held by a trucker who is qualified to drive a double-bottom rig or a set of triples on public roads.
Cf. dual shorts, train, triples.

triaxle: a semi with three rear axles and consequently a greater weight-carrying allowance over a tandem or a single-axle trailer.
Cf. centipede, combinations, tandem spread, three nines.

trip lease: the leasing by an owner-operator to a company on a one-trip basis, contrasted to a lease of a year or more.
Syn.: trippin'.
Cf. broker, cardboard driver, connecting carrier, gypsy, interline, wildcat.

triple deck: to place two trailers (flats, single-drops or lowboys) on top of a third in order to transfer them all to a new location.
Cf. deck, double deck, full mount.

triple mount: a saddle-mount operation in which three tractors are mounted piggyback onto another which acts as the power unit.

Cf. double mount, full mount, saddle mount.

triples: a combination composed of a tractor and three trailers, each of which is shorter than a full-sized semi-trailer. Triples are seen only in the West, where length and weight limitations are up to date.

Cf. double bottom, dual shorts, long double, set of joints, trainman's license, twin trailers.

triplex: a Mack transmission that has two gearshifts for a one-gearbox transmission; the main gearshift lever controls five forward speeds; the auxiliary gearshift controls three additional speeds. In the typical triplex, there are fifteen forward speeds.

Cf. duplex, gearboxes, over and under, quad, three-way split, two-stick transmission, brownie.

trippin': trip leasing a truck to a company.

Cf. cardboard driver, connecting carrier, interline, trip lease, wildcat.

trolley lines: the two air hoses and the electrical cable that run between the tractor and the trailer.

Syn.: trailer connections.

Cf. trolley wire.

trolley-valve handle: the handle in a tractor that activates the trailer's brakes. A trucker might apply the trolley valve when going downhill too fast or in ice and snow to prevent jackknifing. If the trucker applied only the tractor's foot brake in such an instance, he would run the risk of burning out the brakes, failing to slow the rig or having it jackknife. The

trolley-valve handle is named after the lever that motormen used on the old-time trolleys to activate the brakes.
Syn.: hand valve, monkey bar.
Cf. East Coast hookup, jack-off bar, Johnson bar, West Coast hookup.

trolley wire: the electrical cable that runs between the tractor and the trailer.
Syn.: pigtail.
Cf. air hose, handshake, trailer connections, trolley lines.

truck: (noun) **1.** a one-unit motor-powered vehicle, such as a straight job, used for the commercial transport of freight or goods of any and every description. **2.** generally speaking, a tractor-trailer combination.
Syn.: big rig, combinations, oil burner, rig, semi, scow, tandem, tractor-trailer, widow-maker.
Cf. trailer types.
(verb) to drive a tractor-trailer.
Cf. eatin' concrete, grab some gears, herd, make some miles, wheel a rig.

trucker: a man who wheels a rig.
Syn.: commercial tourist, commercial highway engineer, distribution technician, double-clutchin' man, gear jammer, gear shifter, intercity driver, line driver, long-haul driver, over-the-road driver, spinner, turnaround driver, semi driver.
Cf. aviator, boll weevil, clutch artist, cowboy, highballer, lane hopper, lead foot, sheep herder, tailboard artist, truckologist, truck-stop commando.

truck jockey: a trucker who only thinks he can drive well.

Syn.: tailboard artist.

Cf. big rigger, boll weevil, sheep herder, truck-stop commando.

truckologist: **1**. a skilled truck driver.

Cf. clutch artist.

2. derogatorily used, a trucker who brags about his many skills.

Cf. cowboy, sheep herder, tailboard artist, truck jockey, truck-stop commando.

truck-o-tel: a motel or hotel for truck drivers, usually found along truck routes or at large truck stops.

Cf. fuel stop, truck stop.

truck stop: a complex that caters to the needs of the over-the-road driver and his rig. A truck stop usually includes a restaurant, showers, bunk rooms, private rooms, a truckers' store, a garage, a tire service, recreation rooms, lounges, a laundromat and, of course, gas and diesel fuel pumps.

Cf. choke and puke, coffee pot, fuel stop, pig-pen, truck-o-tel, T-five.

truck-stop commando: **1**. a trucker who spends more time outside his truck washing it and shining the chrome than he does inside driving it.

Cf. road bum, rolling palace.

2. a trucker who brags about his driving skill but who is really a mediocre driver.

Syn.: tailboard artist, truck jockey.

Cf. big rigger, truckologist.

truck-tractor: a tractor used to pull a trailer or a

combination of trailers loaded with cargo over the road, as opposed to a farm tractor.
Syn.: horse, power unit.
Cf. semi-trailer, tractor-trailer, truck.

truck-trailer: a combination of a straight truck and a full trailer.
Cf. double-bottom rig, full trailer, semi and pup, semi-trailer, tractor-trailer.

trumpet: a long air horn.
Cf. hoo-hooer.

turbocharger: a type of blower whose purpose is to force air into the intake manifold at higher than atmospheric pressure in order to increase engine power and performance. A turbocharger is similar to two pinwheels connected by a rod. Exhaust gases from the engine strike the first pinwheel, making it revolve. This action rotates the connecting bar and the pinwheel on the other end, and the second pinwheel forces air into the intake manifold.
Cf. blower, oakie blower, supercharger.

turn: to make a round trip to and from a specific city or terminal (as in, "I turned New York three times last week").
Cf. flyer, pull, turn around driver.

turnaround driver: a trucker who commonly runs to one destination and returns to his starting point, as opposed to a trucker with a peddle run or one who does not have scheduled runs. The turnaround point is the most distant place the trucker runs to before returning to his terminal.
Cf. turn.

turn it on: to drive fast.

Syn.: build a fire, burn the rubber, floorboard it, flying low, gettin' stretched, haul the mail, pour on the coals, smokin' in high gear, tacked out.

turnpike tightwad: a lightweight tractor, such as a conventional Chevrolet or Ford. A trucker driving such a tractor hauls a greater payload and may pay lower turnpike tolls than a trucker driving a much heavier tractor.

Cf. moneymaker, poor man's tractor, tightwad tractor.

turn the wick up: **1.** to adjust the fuel pump on an engine so that the engine gets more fuel.

Syn.: open 'er up, set it up.

Cf. cut 'er down, weaned out.

2. to set the hand throttle on an engine so that the engine will idle faster than it would on its own; may be done to make the engine warm up faster or to keep the cab warmer in cold weather while the trucker is parked at a truck stop.

twin chimneys: two smokestacks on a tractor. They enable the engine to "exhale" easier and release the back pressure of the exhaust in the manifold.

Syn.: dual stacks, twin stacks.

Cf. bark, flame thrower, goathorns, gutted, talk.

twin screw: a tractor with a steering axle and two drive axles to the rear, as opposed to a tractor with only one driver and one tag axle.

Syn.: both axles pulling, full screw, tandem drive, two axles pulling.

Cf. bogies, dead axle, drive axle, steering axle, tag axle.

twin spots: **1.** small, round spotlights on a cab. **Syn.**: dual spots.
2. the spotlights on a tractor that are located on the upper front corners of the cab.
Cf. cattle light, horse light, house number hunters, nameplate finders.

twin stacks: two exhaust pipes or smokestacks on a tractor.
Syn.: dual stacks, twin chimneys.
Cf. gutted, smokestack, talk, woodpecker.

twin trailers: a truck combination with one tractor and two trailers.
Syn.: double-bottom rig, doubles, set of joints, twin trailers.
Cf. dual shorts, long double, triples.

two axles pulling: refers to the action of a full- or twin-screw tractor; both rear axles determine the rate of progression.
Syn.: both axles pulling, tandem drive.
Cf. dead axle, drivers, live axle, tag axle.

two-man operation: an operation in which a tractor-trailer or a straight truck with sleeper berth is driven by two drivers who alternate their driving duties.
Cf. single operation.

two-speed axle: a drive axle with a low ratio and a high ratio. In a tractor with a two-speed axle, the driver gets his ten speeds by using one gearshift lever and a five-speed main box. The low and high ranges are not gotten from an auxiliary gearbox but from the rear axle;

the way the driver gets the low and high range is by means of a button on the gearshift lever. For instance, if the truck is in second low, the trucker flips the button up to change to second high; to go to third low, he shifts to third in the main box and pushes the button down again for low range.

Cf. gearboxes, three-speed axle, unishift.

two-speed gloves: gloves worn by a trucker while driving; probably named for the two-speed rear axle that is manually controlled by the driver. By tradition, two-speed gloves are almost always white.

Syn.: split-shiftin' gloves.

Cf. chain-drive pocketbook, double-clutchin' boots, gearshift cap.

two-stick transmission: a truck transmission with two gearshift levers.

Syn.: mix-master special.

Cf. aux box, brownie, duplex, four-by-four, gear boxes, main box, quad, triplex, wobblestick.

two-story Emeryville: manufactured by International Harvester, a conventional cab with the elevation of a cabover. The floor of the cab is removable to permit access to the engine because the cab does not have a tilt mechanism.

Cf. bifocal Internation, corn binder, Emeryville, four thousand, In Hock Constantly, spaceship, West Coast binder.

two-story Falcon: the older model Ford cabover. Probably named by a disgruntled driver.

Cf. corn binder, **F**ix or **R**epair **D**aily, **G**arage **M**an's **C**ompanion, **R**uns **E**mpty **O**nly.

two-way split: a two-speed auxiliary box; so named because, for every gear in the main box, this auxiliary has a low speed and a high speed, or a two-way split in the gears.
Cf. duplex, four-way split, high side, low side, quad, triplex, three-way split, two-stick transmission.

U

unishift: a ten-speed Mack transmission for which there is only one gearshift lever on a five-speed main box; low and high ranges are obtained by manipulating a button on the shift lever. The unishift should be distinguished from a tractor with a two-speed axle because the low and high speeds of the unishift operate from the transmission, not from the rear axle.
Cf. aux box, brownie, gearboxes, main box, three-speed axle, two-speed axle.
Note: The unishift works on the same principle as the Roadranger transmission.

unit: a road horse or tractor; from "power unit."
Cf. loose horse, rolling stock, sick horse, tractor, tractor types.

unlatch: to release the fifth wheel lock preparatory to dropping the trailer.
Syn.: pull the pin.
Cf. break the unit, jump the pin, kingpin, spot the box.

Upjohns: pep pills, such as Dexedrine and Benzedrine.

Syn.: copilots.
Cf. bennie, bennie chaser, helpers, L.A. turnaround.

use the feelers: to drive without lamps or lights.
Cf. bus markers, clearance lights, driving lights, identification lights, running lights, torpedoes, twin spots.

V

van: a trailer of the large, rectangular or "box" variety, as opposed to a lowboy, flat, pole trailer or tanker.
Syn.: box.
Cf. body, drop the box, dry box, semi, spot the box, trailer types.

vanliner: a cabover tractor manufactured by White Freightliner that has a wide (about fifty-four inches) sleeping compartment; it can be custom ordered with many extras and options such as a siren burglar alarm, self-lighting dome lights in the baggage compartment and a clothes compartment at the end of the sleeper—in addition to the many luxurious driver comforts customarily found on owner-operated rigs.
Cf. Fruitliner, Japanese Freightliner, rolling palace.

V.C.R.: the **v**ehicle **c**ondition **r**eport; an I. C. C. requirement for all vehicles under the Commission's jurisdiction. The driver must inspect all parts of his vehicle before and after each trip in order to see that they are safe and to report any problem to his company so that repairs can be made before the vehicle is used again.

Cf. I.C.C., log book.

ventilate the engine: to throw a piston's connecting rod through the side of an engine; the action of the engine.

Cf. broke to lead, peanut roaster, punctured lung, rehaul.

Volkswagen spotter: a West Coast mirror placed by the side vent on the right tractor door whose vent has been replaced with glass; it enables the trucker to see small cars coming up from behind on the right side of the rig.

Cf. cop spotters, defrostos, peek-a-boo mirror, West Coasters.

vulture: a spotter plane that circles over highways in order to observe speeders and lawbreakers; the pilot radios his observations to state troopers in patrol cars.

Cf. believer, big hat, bird dog, gum ball machine, Radar Alley.

W

waffles: nonskid tires.

Cf. baloneys, irons, put on the iron, rubber, sanders.

waterboy: a truck equipped with a tank and spraying devices that are used to spray water or chemicals onto the ground.

water dog: a truck with leaky water lines, requiring frequent refilling.

Cf. punctured lung, slop the hogs.

water-level hauling capacity: the capacity of a dump trailer whose load is level with the top of its sides and is not heaped; expressed in cubic yards.

Cf. bathtub dump, cheater boards, hungry boards, struck capacity.

weaned out: said of an engine in which the proportion of fuel in the air and fuel mixture being burned in the cylinders has been greatly decreased. Large fleets often wean out engines for purposes of fuel economy, especially if they do not care how long it takes their drivers to get from one point to another.

Syn.: cut back, cut 'er down.

Cf. open 'er up, set it up, turn the wick up.

weeder geese hauler: jocularly, an operator who supposedly owns and hauls geese, which he rents to cotton and strawberry farmers so that the geese can eat the weeds around the plants. For instance, when asked what he hauls, a trucker might reply, "Weeder geese," and see how long he could keep his questioner in a state of confusion.

Cf. carrier, painted scrap-iron hauler, shanty hauler, shoat and goat conductor, specialized carrier, steel jockey.

well: the deck part of a lowboy trailer that is lower than the front and rear ends of a double-drop lowboy.

Cf. double deck, level deck lowboy, stretch lowboy.

West Coast binder: an International Harvester

tractor manufactured in their plant in Emeryville, California.

Cf. corn binder, Emeryville, four thousand, spaceship, two-story Emeryville.

West Coasters: short for West Coast mirrors, which are large, rectangular rearview mirrors on a tractor.

Syn.: West Coast mirrors.

Cf. cop spotter, powderpuff, Volkswagen spotter.

West Coast hookup: an I.C.C. requirement, the West Coast hookup is one in which the foot brake activates the brakes of both the tractor and trailer together in order to reduce the probability of jackknifing the rig in a sudden stop or accident.

Cf. East Coast hookup, trolley-valve handle.

West Coast mirrors: large, rectangular rearview mirrors on a tractor. When a trucker maneuvers through a narrow area, West Coast mirrors function like a cat's whiskers: if the mirrors make it through, the rest of the rig will, too.

Syn.: cop spotters, West Coasters.

Cf. blind side, defrostos, peek-a-boo mirrors, powderpuff, Volkswagen spotters.

West Coast rig: a tractor manufactured for use in the West, where high-horsepower rigs are needed to cope with the mountainous terrain. Equipped with a much longer wheelbase than eastern rigs, these trucks can scale a greater weight (based on bridge laws). The length of and distance between the axles are the bases for determining the gross weight, while in the East gross weight is determined by the number of square inches of tire surface.

Cf. axle forward, bridge formula, West Coast tandem.

West Coast spread: a trailer with a separation greater than four feet between the two rear axles, the rearmost of which is located immediately beneath the rear end of the trailer, as opposed to a spread trailer with the axles located further up beneath the body.

Cf. spread, three-legged trailer, three nines, West Coast tandem, wide-spread.

West Coast tandem: a trailer on which the axles are located immediately beneath the rear end of the trailer, as opposed to one with the axles located further up beneath the body.

Cf. sliding tandem, stretched out, West Coast spread.

West Coast turnaround: a strong stay-awake pill; so named because the user can supposedly turn the West Coast without sleeping.

Syn.: L.A. turnaround.

Cf. beaned up, bennie, copilots, helpers, Upjohns.

wet line kit: the hydraulic storage tank and pump that operate the hoist system on a dump trailer.

Cf. dump body.

wet lines: hydraulic lines that extend from a tractor's hydraulic reservoir to the hoist system on its trailer.

Cf. quick-disconnect couplers, tipper, wet line kit.

whalenose: an old Diamond-T conventional model tractor with a long hood.

Cf. bonnet, long-nose.

wheel a rig: to drive a truck.

Syn.: herd, push a rig.

Cf. big hole it, eatin' concrete, foot in the floorboards, grab some gears, make some miles.

whippletree: the coupling device that connects the first and second trailers in a double-bottom rig.

Syn.: converter dolly, double hookup, jo-jo.

Cf. Jifflox dolly, kite without a tail, tongue.

whistler: a police car, esp. with its siren on.

whistlin' gear: the highest combination of gears in a tractor's transmission; may have been named for the whistling sound older tractors made when in overdrive gear, or for the possibility that a rig traveling in this gear could attract the attention of a "whistler"—a police car.

Syn.: big hole, go-away gear, goin' home gear, pay hole.

Cf. birddog, believer, bubble gum machine.

white collar man: a driver who handles clean merchandise only.

Cf. chimney sweep run, fingerprint, trucker.

wide-spread: refers to trailer axles that are more than eight feet apart.

Cf. Michigan spread, Ohio spread, spread, tandem spread, three-legged trailer, West Coast spread.

widow-maker: any tractor-trailer, diesel truck or big rig.
Syn.: diesel, horse, oil burner, rig, semi, tandem.
Cf. truck.

wildcat: an owner-operator who contracts independently with various shippers to haul consignments. He is his own boss, does not work out of a company and rarely makes the same run twice.
Syn.: gypsy, gray operator, moonlighter, wildcatter.
Cf. boondockin', broker, Moonlight Express, runnin' hot.

wildcatter: an owner-operator who contracts independently with various shippers to haul consignments. He is his own boss, does not work out of a company (and thus lacks federally granted authority) and rarely makes the same run twice.
Syn.: gray operator, gypsy, moonlighter, wildcat.
Cf. boondockin', Moonlight Express.

winch rig: a tractor with a hoist or winch.
Cf. float, gin poles, mud trailer, split-shaft PTO.

wind 'er up: **1.** to start a truck.
Syn.: build a fire, fire it up, kick 'er over, shake down the ashes.
2. to crank a starter in an old-time truck (obsolete).
Cf. stew winder.
3. to speed up a truck.

Syn.: haul the mail, pour on the coals.
Cf. tacked out.

windmill: a truck is said to windmill when the top r.p.m. of the engine is run up against the governor of the fuel pump without picking up any speed.
Cf. drag down, grab one, keep 'er winding, overspeed.

windshield wiper-itis: jocularly, the mythical affliction of a trucker who has been driving in the rain for several days: when he stops and goes into a truck stop, his head still follows the motions of the windshield wipers.
Cf. fair-weather driver, sunshine driver.

winter front: the covering that truckers sometimes place over the grill of the tractor in an effort to keep the interior of the cab warmer during the winter. Regular winter fronts are usually made out of a heavy-duty tarp, although a chilly trucker may improvise with anything from cardboard to Navajo blankets.
Syn.: bandaids, diapers.
Cf. bandaged up, pneumonia sedan, shutters.

wobblers: spoke wheels; so named because they are difficult to keep aligned.
Syn. Dayton wheels, manure-spreader wheels, square wheels.
Cf. babymoon hubcaps, Budd wheels.

wobblestick: the shift lever on a gearbox.
Syn.: mixing stick.
Cf. aux box, brownie, gearboxes, main box, mix-master special, two-stick transmission.

wobbly hole: neutral gear.

Cf. eleventh gear, Mexican overdrive, midnight overdrive, thirteenth gear, wobblestick.

wood pecker: a weighted and hinged cover used to keep water from entering the exhaust pipe (smokestack) of a rig. When the truck is in motion, the hinge opens because of pressure from the exhaust; when the ignition is shut off, the cover rests over the opening.

Syn.: Bob White, butterfly.

Cf. flame thrower.

working for Standard Oil: said of a trucker who drives a rig that burns fuel or oil in excess.

Cf. bubble burner, diesel, gas job, juice jockey, oil burner, smoker.

wrap 'er around the bend: to skid around a turn.

Cf. bite a turn, chop a turn, need a hinge, split-arc.

Y

yard bird: a driver who spots trailers and moves vehicles around a terminal yard.

Syn.: spotter, yard man.

Cf. shagging, spot the body, yard mule.

yard man: a terminal worker who spots or parks trucks.

Syn.: spotter, yard bird.

Cf. doodle-bug, shagging, spotter, spot the body, swamper, yard mule.

yard mule: a small tractor used to relocate semitrailers in a truck yard or terminal.

Cf. dock walloper, mule, spot the box, yard bird.

Z

zebra stripes: decorative stripes on a tractor's bumper.

Cf. all dolled up, Christmas tree, decked out, floating chrome, goodied up, hillbilly chrome, rolling palace.

zephyr haul: a shipment of lightweight cargo.

Syn.: balloon freight, load of wind.

Cf. feather hauler, load of postholes.

Montie Tak spends most of her time on the road. Since graduating from Dickinson College in Carlisle, Pennsylvania, she has driven trucks from coast to coast many times and is now an owner-operator. She spent several years collecting the in-language of the trucking industry by listening to the talk of drivers across the country and recording their speech at every opportunity. When she is not at the wheel of her big Mack, she writes poetry and pursues her interest in the other kind of horsepower in the countryside around, Newville, Pennsylvania.